CULINARY CLASSICS FROM

Beachside to Boardwalk

A Collection of Recipes from
The Junior League of Galveston County, Inc.

CULINARY CLASSICS FROM

Beachside to Boardwalk

Published by The Junior League of Galveston County, Inc.
Copyright © 2010 by
The Junior League of Galveston County, Inc.
210 Kempner Avenue
Galveston, Texas 77550
409-765-7646
www.jlgalveston.org

Photography © by Abbey Hanson

Library of Congress Control Number: 2010922698
ISBN: 978-0-615-32379-4

This cookbook is a collection of our favorite recipes, which are not necessarily original recipes.

Edited, Designed, and Produced by

 Favorite Recipes® Press

an imprint of

FRP.INC

a wholly owned subsidiary of Southwestern/Great American, Inc.
P.O. Box 305142
Nashville, Tennessee 37230
1-800-358-0560

Art Director and Book Design: Steve Newman
Project Editor: Tanis Westbrook

Manufactured in the United States of America
First Printing 2010
10,000 copies

Beachside to Boardwalk Committee

2007–2010 COMMITTEE

Erin Kearney Conrad, Cookbook Chairman 2009–2010
Cara Koza, Cookbook Chairman 2008–2009
Michele Hay, Cookbook Chairman 2006–2008
Raegan Markey, Cookbook Co-Chairman 2008–2010

Larissa Botik
Jennifer Caffey
Debbie Candelari
Linda Dolfi
Jennifer Dunne Burnett
Ashlee Dupont
Dedra Etzel
Abbie Hanson
Amanda Hawes

Joanne Hlavenka
Michelle Holland
Rebecca Jaworski
Terry Lynn Jones
Jill Kaale
Jessica Martinez
Kathryn Mixon
Joy Nagel
Kelly Parks
Holly Pelletier

Erin Piazza
Kimberly Primm
Cassandra Pruitt
Arminda Scarborough
Heidi Seigel
Annie Stephens
Kerri Sweeney
Stephanie Vasut
Lauraleigh Gourley Vogel

EXECUTIVE COMMITTEE

Michele Hay, President 2009–2010
Marjorie Kovacevich, President 2008–2009
Kelly Johns, President 2007–2008
Libbie Ansell, President 2006–2007

About The Junior League of Galveston County, Inc.

MISSION

The Junior League of Galveston, Inc., is an organization committed to promoting volunteerism, developing the potential of women, and improving communities through the effective action and leadership of trained volunteers. Its purpose is exclusively educational and charitable.

The Junior League of Galveston County, Inc., seeks the support of conscientious residents and business owners who want to see our community improve through our projects and community programs.

SERVICE PROJECTS

Over the past fifty-eight years the women of the Junior League of Galveston County, Inc., have served our area with over 13,000 dedicated volunteer hours each year. Some of these projects include Reading Is Fundamental, Stuff the Bus, Creating Connections, Girls on the Run, Habitat for Humanity, Jr. Junior Leaguers, Kids in the Kitchen, Special People's Ball, Relay for Life, Pedi Pals Program, and D'Feet Breast Cancer. We also provide a scholarship assistance award for college-bound women of Galveston County. Lastly, our Community Assistance Fund benefits organizations like the Salvation Army, Jesse Tree, Women's Resource and Crisis Center, The Advocacy Center for Children, and many others.

PUBLICATIONS

Culinary Classics from Beachside to Boardwalk is The Junior League of Galveston County, Inc.'s, new addition to our cookbook collection. We are very proud of this cookbook because it encompasses a great deal of time, effort, and collaboration on the part of the League as a whole. The first cookbook, *Rare Collections*, was published in 1985. It was successfully reprinted five times and sold over 55,000 copies.

Preface

Over the past fifty-eight years the impact The Junior League of Galveston County has had on the community has been made possible by hundreds of talented women who seek to actively serve others through the giving of their time and respective talents. The Junior League of Galveston County supplies over 13,000 volunteer hours each year to meet the continuously evolving needs of their diverse community through a myriad of services including the areas of literacy, self-awareness education, and the promotion of healthy lifestyle choices for children.

It is through the tireless efforts and contributions of JLGC members that initiatives were begun to benefit local agencies and programs such as Reading Is Fundamental, Jr. Junior Leaguers, Kids in the Kitchen, Habitat for Humanity, Pedi-Pals at the University of Texas Medical Branch Hospital, Girls on the Run, and Creating Connections at The Children's Center.

In addition to the support offered by its members, The Junior League of Galveston County is fortified by the generous support of nonprofit organizations, private donors, and various community partnerships within Galveston County. Such efforts allow for the creation of education scholarships that benefit college-bound women of Galveston County. Through the Community Assistance Fund, the League provides financial assistance to local charities and organizations such as The Ronald McDonald House Endowment, Salvation Army, The Advocacy Center for Children, and the Women's Resource and Crisis Center.

The great need for donor resources and the positive impact they have were realized during the devastating aftermath of Hurricane Ike. The Junior League of Galveston County mounted a swift campaign to raise awareness of the needs of those impacted by the hurricane on Galveston Island and its surrounding areas. Efforts ranged from organizing clothing drives at local churches, to performing countless hours of post-Ike cleanup efforts, and included collecting nonperishable food items to replenish county-wide food pantry needs. It is during challenging times such as this that the League's commitment to improving their community through effective action and promotion of volunteerism is realized.

Certainly many hours of consideration and careful planning have preceded the publication of *Beachside to Boardwalk*. It is filled with historic details and anecdotes which fill the reader with a true sense of all that Galveston County embodies and has to offer. As you enjoy this collection of treasured recipes, you should know that your support will benefit this community by helping to further the long-term goal of The Junior League of Galveston County for years to come.

Sponsors

We would like to express our deepest gratitude to the following for their kind contributions. Their generosity allowed for the first printing of *Culinary Classics from Beachside to Boardwalk* and is greatly appreciated by The Junior League of Galveston County, Inc.

Lawrence R. Clarke, M.D.

Valeria Clarke

James Grant, M.D.

Abbey Hanson

Malloy and Son Funeral Home

Introduction

Welcome to *Beachside to Boardwalk*. The Junior League of Galveston County is proud to introduce this collection of recipes. Some have been passed down from memory through generations of "a dash of this and a dab of that," while others bring the fresh new twists and creative spins of today.

Galveston County is dripping with Southern Texas hospitality. As you indulge in our time-tested, crowd-pleasing, party-worthy recipes, we hope you will take a second to read a little about our history, and get lost in the beautiful imagery that goes with it. Whether we are taking a stroll down Main Street in League City or riding a carriage on the Strand, we do it all in our own style, and our cooking is no different. One morning we could go out and catch the biggest Gulf shrimp around, and that night have an elegant soiree for our friends and family.

Some would say we are a little more reflective now than once upon a time. As we were preparing this cookbook, Hurricane Ike reared his head on our coast, bringing devastation and turmoil. Some areas of Galveston were completely unrecognizable, while others survived, but with bumps and bruises. Naturally, we pulled ourselves up by the bootstraps and quickly got to work on our battered homes, parks, and spirits. The women of The Junior League of Galveston County played an integral part in volunteer efforts, making the League's mission "Survive, Revive, Thrive." As a result, our pride has grown immeasurably as we continue to rebuild our county, and we are exceptionally proud of our Southeast Texas home.

As you travel through this book, you will discover delicious recipes that bring family and friends together. Rise and Shine with us, and get your day started with brunch. Join in the festivities of Galveston with Tantalizing Tidbits. Keep it Light and Breezy with soups and salads. Journey through various Galveston parks and get a taste of Birds of a Feather. Of course, you'll want to sample Divine Red and White with our beef, pork, and wild game. Grab a Catch of the Coast and put the finishing touches to your meals with Coastal Complements. Naturally, the end is ever so sweet with our Lasting Impressions desserts.

Beachside to Boardwalk is a work of heart, capturing the recipes, stories, and photographs of Galveston County, the place we call "home." We hope you enjoy these delectable dishes and sumptuous treats, as they will surely delight for generations to come.

TABLE OF CONTENTS

Divine Red and White

Catch of the Coast

Coastal Complements

Lasting Impressions

Rise and Shine

BRUNCH

In Galveston, Texas, merriment is our calling card. In lieu of honking taxis and angry buses, we get to wake up every day to the soft sounds of the gulf's breeze. Blue skies are a frequent forecast, making us happier than most. Around here, we wave at each other, we smile at strangers, and we mind our manners.

While we spend our days in warm sunshine, we have certainly had our fair share of natural disasters. The 1900 Storm and hurricanes Carla, Alicia, and Ike ripped through our island, though we still stand strong today. It takes more than hurricanes to knock our spirit, and a morning stroll down the Seawall will show just that. Take a walk early one day and remember Murdoch's Bathhouse, with its blue exterior and white seashells. Dream about what it would have been like to see Frank Sinatra sing at the famed Balinese Room.

However you choose to Rise and Shine, do it with gusto as we do here, and let us offer you a few delectable eats, with Galveston flair, that will give any day a jump start.

MILLER'S
SEAWALL GRILL
SINCE 1976

1824 SEAWALL
GALVESTON, TEXAS

sponsor

Sweet Cheese Pancakes

Sweet Cheese Filling	1 egg white
8 ounces mascarpone cheese	3/4 cup milk
1 tablespoon honey	1 egg yolk
1 tablespoon milk	2 teaspoons walnut oil or hazelnut oil
1/2 teaspoon finely shredded lemon zest	1 1/2 teaspoons granulated sugar
1/4 teaspoon anise seeds, crushed	1/2 teaspoon vanilla extract

Pancakes	Assembly
3/4 cup all-purpose flour	1 cup seedless green grapes, sliced
1/2 teaspoon baking powder	3/4 cup confectioners' sugar

To prepare the filling, beat the mascarpone cheese, honey, milk, lemon zest and anise seeds in a bowl until blended. Cover and set aside.

To prepare the pancakes, mix the flour and baking powder together. Beat the egg white at high speed in a small mixing bowl until soft peaks form. Combine the milk, egg yolk, walnut oil, granulated sugar and vanilla in a large mixing bowl and beat well. Add the flour mixture and beat until smooth. Fold in the beaten egg white until the mixture is the consistency of a milk shake. Spray a nonstick griddle or skillet with nonstick cooking spray. Heat over medium heat for 1 to 2 minutes. Pour 2 tablespoons of the batter onto the griddle and quickly spread into a 4- to 5-inch circle. Cook for 20 seconds or until light brown. Turn gently with a spatula and cook for 15 seconds. Invert onto a plate lined with paper towels. Repeat with the remaining batter, placing a dry paper towel between each pancake. Cover and keep warm.

To assemble and serve, spoon 1 slightly rounded tablespoon of the cheese filling across each pancake just below the center. Fold the bottom of each pancake over the filling. Fold in the sides and roll up. Arrange seam side down on individual dessert plates. Top with the grapes and sprinkle with the confectioners' sugar. Serve warm or at room temperature.

Serves 10 to 12

Pumpkin Ginger Waffles

3 tablespoons unsalted butter

1 1/4 cups all-purpose flour

1 1/2 teaspoons baking powder

1/2 teaspoon baking soda

1/4 teaspoon salt

2 teaspoons ground ginger

1/2 teaspoon cinnamon

1/4 cup finely chopped crystallized ginger

2 eggs

3/4 cup buttermilk

1/2 cup canned pumpkin purée

1/2 cup sugar

3/4 teaspoon vanilla extract

Melt the butter in a saucepan over medium heat. Remove from the heat to cool. Mix the flour, baking powder, baking soda, salt, ground ginger and cinnamon in a large bowl. Toss 2 tablespoons of the flour mixture with the crystallized ginger in a small bowl and set aside. Whisk the eggs, buttermilk, pumpkin purée, sugar and vanilla in a medium bowl until smooth. Add the remaining flour mixture and mix well. Stir in the butter. Fold in the crystallized ginger mixture. Do not overmix. Pour 1/2 cup of the batter at a time onto a hot waffle iron. Bake until brown. Keep warm in a preheated 200-degree oven until serving time.

Serves 4 to 6

Overnight Coffee Cake

3 cups all-purpose flour

1 1/2 teaspoons baking powder

1 1/2 teaspoons baking soda

1 cup (2 sticks) butter, softened

1 1/4 cups granulated sugar

3 eggs

15 ounces ricotta cheese

1 cup chopped nuts

1/2 cup packed brown sugar

1 tablespoon cinnamon

1 teaspoon nutmeg

Mix the flour, baking powder and baking soda in a bowl. Beat the butter at high speed in a mixing bowl for 30 seconds. Add the granulated sugar and beat well. Add the eggs one at a time, beating well after each addition. Beat in the ricotta cheese. Stir in the flour mixture. The batter will be very thick. Spread in a greased 9×13-inch baking pan. Mix the nuts, brown sugar, cinnamon and nutmeg in a bowl. Sprinkle evenly over the batter. Chill, covered, for up to 24 hours. Bake in a preheated 350-degree oven for 35 to 40 minutes or until golden brown. Cool slightly before serving.

Serves 15

Nutty French Toast

French Toast
1/4 cup (1/2 stick) butter, softened
12 (3/4-inch) slices bread
6 eggs
1 1/2 cups milk
1/4 cup granulated sugar
2 tablespoons maple syrup
1 teaspoon vanilla extract
1/2 teaspoon salt
2 tablespoons confectioners' sugar

Walnut Maple Syrup
2 cups maple syrup
1 cup walnuts, toasted and chopped
2 tablespoons butter

To prepare the French toast, coat the bottom of a 9×13-inch baking pan with the butter. Arrange the bread in the prepared pan. Beat the eggs, milk, granulated sugar, maple syrup, vanilla and salt in a large bowl and mix well. Pour over the bread. Let stand for 10 minutes. Turn the bread to coat the remaining side. Chill, covered with plastic wrap, for 8 to 10 hours. Arrange the bread slices in a single layer on a baking sheet. Bake in a preheated 400-degree oven for 10 to 15 minutes or until golden brown, turning once. Place on individual serving plates and sprinkle with the confectioners' sugar.

To prepare the syrup, bring the maple syrup, walnuts and butter to a simmer in a heavy medium saucepan. Spoon over the French toast and serve.

Serves 6 to 8

French Toast Casserole

1 loaf bread, thinly sliced

8 eggs, well beaten

1 cup milk

2 cups cream

Pinch of salt

2 tablespoons granulated sugar

1/4 teaspoon nutmeg

1/4 teaspoon cinnamon

1 teaspoon vanilla extract

1 cup packed brown sugar

2 tablespoons corn syrup

1/2 teaspoon nutmeg

1/2 teaspoon cinnamon

1 cup (2 sticks) butter, softened

1 cup chopped pecans

Layer the bread in a buttered 9×13-inch glass baking dish. Combine the eggs, milk, cream, salt, granulated sugar, 1/4 teaspoon nutmeg, 1/4 teaspoon cinnamon and the vanilla in a bowl and blend well. Pour over the bread. Chill, covered with foil, for 8 to 10 hours. Mix the brown sugar, corn syrup, 1/2 teaspoon nutmeg, 1/2 teaspoon cinnamon, the butter and pecans in a bowl. Spread over the bread mixture. Bake in a preheated 350-degree oven for 35 to 40 minutes or until brown and bubbly. Serve with maple syrup, confectioners' sugar and/or fresh fruit.

Serves 8 to 10

GALVESTON ISLAND

Galveston is believed to be five thousand years old and has an interesting history dating over the last five hundred years. In 1817 the Lafitte brothers, fleeing the prosecution of pirates, established a government with visions of creating a "Manhattan on the Gulf." In 1839 Galveston was the most active port west of New Orleans and the largest city in Texas. The island was also home to the state's first post office, hospital, golf course, and opera house.

Cranberry Orange Scones

2 cups all-purpose flour
1 tablespoon baking powder
1/4 cup sugar
1/2 teaspoon salt
1/4 cup (1/2 stick) butter
2 eggs
1/2 cup heavy cream
1 cup cranberries
1 tablespoon grated orange zest
1 egg white, beaten
1/4 cup sugar

Grease a baking sheet with butter or shortening or line with baking parchment or a silicone baking mat. Mix the flour, baking powder, 1/4 cup sugar and the salt in a large mixing bowl. Cut in the butter until crumbly. Beat 2 eggs in a bowl. Stir in the cream. Add to the flour mixture and mix well. Stir in the cranberries and orange zest. Press into a mound on a floured board, adding additional cream, milk or water 1 tablespoon at a time until the mixture holds together if needed. Do not overwork the dough.

Roll the dough into a circle 1-inch thick. Cut into rounds with a fluted pastry cutter. Place on the prepared baking sheet. Brush with the egg white and sprinkle with 1/4 cup sugar. Bake in a preheated 400-degree oven for 15 minutes or until golden brown.

Makes 8 to 12 scones

Blueberry Scones

2 cups all-purpose flour

¼ cup packed brown sugar

1 tablespoon baking powder

¼ teaspoon salt

1 teaspoon fresh lemon zest

¼ cup (½ stick) butter, chilled

1 cup fresh blueberries

¾ cup half-and-half

1 egg

Mix the flour, brown sugar, baking powder, salt and lemon zest in a bowl. Cut in the butter until crumbly. Add the blueberries and toss to mix. Beat the half-and-half and egg in a bowl until smooth. Add to the flour mixture gradually, stirring constantly with a rubber spatula to form a dough. Knead on a lightly floured surface three or four times or until the mixture holds together. Do not overhandle the dough.

Divide the dough into two equal portions. Shape each portion into a 6-inch circle. Cut each circle into six wedges. Place on an ungreased baking sheet. Bake in a preheated 375-degree oven for 20 minutes or until light brown. Serve warm.

Makes 1 dozen

Maple Cream Coffee Treats

1 cup packed brown sugar

½ cup chopped pecans

⅓ cup maple syrup

¼ cup (½ stick) butter, melted

8 ounces cream cheese, softened

¼ cup confectioners' sugar

2 tablespoons butter, softened

2 (10-count) cans flaky biscuits

Combine the brown sugar, pecans, maple syrup and ¼ cup butter in a bowl and stir until smooth. Pour into a 9×13-inch baking dish. Combine the cream cheese, confectioners' sugar and 2 tablespoons butter in a mixing bowl and beat until blended.

Separate the biscuits. Press each biscuit into a 3- to 4-inch circle. Spoon about 1 tablespoon of the cream cheese mixture onto the center of each biscuit. Roll to enclose the filling. Arrange the biscuit rolls seam side down in two rows of ten each in the prepared baking dish. Bake in a preheated 375-degree oven for 25 to 30 minutes or until golden brown. Cool in the pan for 3 minutes. Remove to a serving plate or place on waxed paper to cool completely.

Serves 8 to 10

Kahlúa Brie

1 (14-ounce) wheel Brie cheese
1 tablespoon butter
1 cup finely chopped pecans, toasted
1/3 cup Kahlúa
1/4 cup packed brown sugar

Remove the rind from the top of the cheese and place the cheese on a microwave-safe serving platter. Melt the butter in a saucepan. Stir in the pecans. Cook over medium heat for 5 minutes, stirring constantly. Stir in the Kahlúa and brown sugar. Spoon over the cheese, spreading to the edge. Microwave on High for 1 minute or until hot and bubbly. Serve with melba toast.

Serves 8

Cucumber Tea Sandwiches

8 ounces cream cheese, softened
1/2 cup mayonnaise
1 envelope Italian-style salad dressing mix
1 loaf party rye bread, or 1 French baguette, sliced
2 cucumbers, sliced
Dried dill weed

Combine the cream cheese, mayonnaise and salad dressing mix in a bowl and mix well. Chill, covered, for 6 to 10 hours. Spread the cream cheese mixture evenly over one side of each bread slice. Top each with a cucumber slice. Sprinkle each with a pinch of dill weed.

Serves about 26

Spicy Cheese Sandwiches

1 1/2 cups (3 sticks) butter or margarine, softened
1 1/2 teaspoons Worcestershire sauce
1 1/4 teaspoons dill weed
1 teaspoon onion powder

1 teaspoon garlic salt
3/4 teaspoon Tabasco sauce
Dash of cayenne pepper
1 pound sharp Cheddar cheese, shredded
2 loaves thinly sliced bread, trimmed

Combine the butter, Worcestershire sauce, dill weed, onion powder, garlic salt, Tabasco sauce, cayenne pepper and cheese in a bowl and mix well. For each sandwich, stack three bread slices together. Spread the cheese mixture between each layer. Cut each sandwich into quarters. Place on a baking sheet without the edges touching. Freeze and then wrap in foil. Return to the freezer until serving time. To serve, unwrap the frozen sandwiches and place on a baking sheet. Bake in a preheated 350-degree oven for 20 minutes.

Makes 64 sandwiches

Zucchini Squares

1 cup buttermilk baking mix
1/2 cup (2 ounces) grated Parmesan cheese
3 tablespoons chopped parsley
1/2 teaspoon salt
1/2 teaspoon oregano

1/2 teaspoon pepper
1/2 cup vegetable oil
4 eggs, lightly beaten
3 cups thinly sliced zucchini
3/4 cup finely chopped onion
2 garlic cloves, finely chopped

Combine the baking mix, cheese, parsley, salt, oregano, pepper, oil and eggs in a bowl and mix well. Stir in the zucchini, onion and garlic. Spread in a greased 9×13-inch baking pan. Bake in a preheated 350-degree oven for 35 minutes. Cut into squares. These freeze well and can be made in advance.

Serves 20

Poached Eggs with Spinach and Bacon

1 cup olive oil

2 garlic cloves, crushed

1 tablespoon chopped fresh thyme

1 teaspoon dried crushed red pepper

Salt and black pepper to taste

1 (16-ounce) loaf sourdough bread

2 tablespoons olive oil

2 tablespoons minced shallots

10 ounces fresh baby spinach

1 tablespoon white vinegar

$1/2$ teaspoon salt

4 eggs

8 slices thick bacon, crisp-cooked and cut into halves

Grated Parmesan cheese to taste

Mix 1 cup olive oil, the garlic, thyme and red pepper in a small saucepan. Cook over medium heat for 2 minutes. Remove from the heat. Add salt and black pepper to taste. Trim the crust from the top and sides of the bread, leaving a small crust on the bottom. Cut the loaf into four thick slices. Hollow out the center of each slice, leaving a $3/4$-inch base and $1/2$ inch around the sides. Place on a baking sheet. Brush with the olive oil mixture. Bake in a preheated 425-degree oven for 7 minutes or until golden brown. Remove from the oven to cool. Maintain the oven temperature.

Heat 2 tablespoons olive oil in a large skillet over medium heat. Add the shallots and sauté for 2 minutes. Add the spinach and sauté until wilted. Fill a large skillet with water to $1/2$ inch from the top. Add the vinegar and $1/2$ teaspoon salt. Bring to a boil over medium-high heat. Break one egg into a small custard cup, being careful to keep the yolk intact. Gently slide the egg into the boiling water. Repeat with the remaining eggs. Simmer for 3 minutes for soft cooked or longer.

Fill each bread center with the spinach and top each with four bacon halves. Bake for 5 minutes or until heated through. Place on individual serving plates. Place one poached egg on top of each using a slotted spoon. Add salt and black pepper to taste. Sprinkle with Parmesan cheese.

Serves 4

Smoked Salmon with Eggs Benedict and Dill Hollandaise Sauce

Dill Hollandaise Sauce

1 cup (2 sticks) unsalted butter, softened

1 bunch fresh dill weed

3 egg yolks

2 tablespoons water

1/8 teaspoon kosher salt, or to taste

1/8 teaspoon pepper, or to taste

1 teaspoon Worcestershire sauce

1 teaspoon Tabasco sauce

1/4 teaspoon fresh lemon juice

Eggs Benedict

1/4 cup white vinegar

12 eggs

6 large croissants, cut into halves and lightly toasted

8 ounces sliced smoked salmon

To prepare the sauce, melt the butter in a saucepan over low heat and set aside. Reserve six dill sprigs for garnish and finely chop the remaining dill weed. Fill a saucepan halfway with water. Bring to a gentle simmer over medium-low heat. Place the egg yolks and 2 tablespoons water in a heatproof bowl and set 2 inches above the simmering water. Add 1/8 teaspoon kosher salt and 1/8 teaspoon pepper. Whisk for 5 minutes or just until the mixture begins to thicken. Remove the bowl from the saucepan. Whisk the warm melted butter into the thickened egg yolks a small amount at a time. Add the Worcestershire sauce, Tabasco sauce, lemon juice and chopped dill weed. Season with kosher salt and pepper to taste. Keep warm.

To prepare the eggs Benedict, fill a large shallow saucepan with water to a depth of 2 inches. Bring to a simmer and add the vinegar. Crack six of the eggs one at a time and gently slide into the simmering water. Poach for 4 minutes or until the whites are set and the yolks are glazed but still soft. Remove the eggs carefully with a slotted spoon to a large plate. Repeat with the remaining six eggs. If the eggs cool before serving, reheat in the hot water or in a preheated 250-degree oven for 5 minutes.

To serve, gently blot the eggs with a paper towel to remove any excess water. Place one split croissant cut-side up on each serving plate. Cover generously with the smoked salmon. Place a warm poached egg on each croissant half and cover with the sauce. Garnish with the reserved dill sprigs.

Serves 6

Pesto Ricotta Pie

Pesto

7 1/2 cups basil leaves

1 1/2 cups extra-virgin olive oil

3 garlic cloves

1 teaspoon coarse salt

1/2 teaspoon pepper

3/4 cup pine nuts, toasted

3/4 cup (3 ounces) grated
Parmesan cheese

Pie

2 tablespoons butter

1 large leek, trimmed, rinsed and
thinly sliced

2 eggs

2 egg whites

1/4 cup cream

1 cup ricotta cheese

1/2 cup (2 ounces) grated
Parmesan cheese

2 tablespoons finely chopped fresh
parsley leaves

1/4 teaspoon salt

1/4 teaspoon pepper

8 sheets phyllo dough

1/4 cup (1/2 stick) butter, melted

To prepare the pesto, purée the basil, olive oil, garlic, salt and pepper in a food processor. Add the pine nuts and cheese and process until the pine nuts are chopped.

To prepare the pie, melt 2 tablespoons butter in a medium skillet over medium-high heat. Add the leek. Cook for 5 to 7 minutes or until tender, stirring frequently. Remove to a large bowl and let stand until cool. Whisk the eggs, egg whites and cream in a medium bowl. Add the leek, ricotta cheese, Parmesan cheese, pesto, parsley, salt and pepper and mix well. Lay one sheet of the phyllo dough in a lightly buttered 9-inch pie plate. Brush with the melted butter to within 1 1/2 inches of the edges. Repeat with the remaining phyllo sheets, brushing each layer with melted butter. Trim the edges to conform to the shape of the pie plate with kitchen shears. Pour in the pesto mixture. Brush the edge of the phyllo with the remaining melted butter. Bake in a preheated 375-degree oven for 40 minutes or until the edge is golden brown and the filling is set. Cool before serving.

Serves 6

Rosemary Potato Frittata

4 ounces tiny new potatoes, cut into 1/4-inch slices
1/4 cup chopped red onion
1/4 cup chopped yellow bell pepper
1 tablespoon butter
4 medium eggs, beaten
1/2 teaspoon chopped fresh rosemary
1/8 teaspoon salt
1/4 cup (1 ounce) shredded Swiss cheese
1/8 teaspoon cracked pepper

Combine the potatoes and onion with a small amount of boiling water in a medium nonstick skillet. Cook, covered, for 7 minutes. Add the bell pepper. Cook, covered, for 3 to 5 minutes or until the vegetables are tender. Drain the vegetables in a colander. Cool and dry the skillet.

Melt the butter in the skillet over medium heat. Return the vegetables to the skillet. Whisk the eggs, rosemary and salt in a small bowl. Pour over the vegetables. Cook over medium heat, lifting the edge gently with a spatula as the eggs set to allow the uncooked eggs to flow underneath; do not stir. Continue cooking and lifting the egg mixture until nearly set and the top is moist. Remove from the heat. Sprinkle with the cheese. Let stand, covered, for 3 to 4 minutes or until the top is set and the cheese melts. Sprinkle with the pepper.

Serves 2 to 4

MURDOCH'S

Murdoch's Bathhouse is another one of Galveston's most historic locations. Bathhouses were very popular in the early 1900s, and their purpose was renting bathing suits and providing showers for beach visitors. Murdoch's was built in the late 1800s directly on the sand and became a souvenir and gift shop in 1910. Today, Murdoch's is built on pilings over the Gulf of Mexico and offers wonderful souvenirs for Galveston tourists.

The Seawall is a seven-mile-long and seventeen-foot-high wall of concrete built along the coast of Galveston for protection against storm surges from hurricanes. The idea was conceived after the 1900 Storm battered Galveston and killed more than 6,000 people. When the city was rebuilt, the grade of the town was raised and the Seawall was constructed. Since its creation, the Seawall has withstood a number of violent hurricanes.

Coastal Quiche Florentine

4 eggs
1 cup half-and-half
1/2 cup mayonnaise
2 tablespoon all-purpose flour
1/3 cup minced onion
Salt and garlic powder to taste
8 ounces sharp Cheddar cheese, shredded
1 (10-ounce) package frozen chopped spinach,
thawed and drained
1 unbaked (9-inch) pie shell

Combine the eggs, half-and-half, mayonnaise and flour in a medium bowl and stir to mix well. Add the onion, salt, garlic powder, cheese and spinach and mix well. Pour into the pie shell. Bake in a preheated 350-degree oven for 50 minutes or until the top is golden brown.

For **Bacon Asparagus Swiss Quiche**, substitute 1 pound asparagus, trimmed and steamed, for the spinach, Swiss cheese for the Cheddar cheese and add 6 slices crisp-cooked bacon, crumbled.

Serves 6 to 8

Cheesy Grits Soufflé

1 cup grits
4 cups boiling water
1 teaspoon salt
2 cups (8 ounces) shredded sharp
Cheddar cheese
1/2 cup chopped onion

1 garlic clove, crushed
2 tablespoons butter, melted
1/3 cup finely chopped jalapeño chiles
4 egg yolks
4 egg whites, stiffly beaten

Stir the grits into the boiling water in a saucepan. Add the salt. Cook over medium heat for 10 to 20 minutes or until thickened, stirring frequently. Remove from the heat. Stir in the cheese until melted. Sauté the onion and garlic in the butter in a skillet over medium to high heat for 5 minutes. Add to the grits. Stir in the jalapeño chiles. Stir a small amount of the hot grits mixture into the egg yolks. Stir the egg yolks into the grits mixture. Fold in the egg whites. Spoon into a greased 2-quart baking dish. Bake in a preheated 350-degree oven for 45 to 50 minutes or until set.

Serves 6 to 8

Cheesy Sourdough Breakfast Bake

1/2 (11/2-pound) loaf sourdough bread
1/2 cup (1 stick) butter, melted
1/8 teaspoon garlic powder
8 ounces sharp Cheddar
cheese, shredded

8 ounces mild Cheddar cheese, shredded
6 eggs, beaten
3 cups milk
12 ounces bacon, crisp-cooked and
crumbled (optional)

Cut the bread into cubes the size of croutons. Mix the butter and garlic powder in a bowl. Add the bread cubes and toss to coat. Place in a 9×13-inch baking dish. Layer the cheese over the bread cubes. Whisk the eggs and milk in a bowl. Pour over the cheese. Chill for 8 to 10 hours. Bake in a preheated 325-degree oven for 45 minutes, sprinkling with the bacon during the last 15 minutes.

Serves 8 to 10

Ham Asparagus Strata

1 1/2 tablespoons butter
4 cups (bite-size) pieces English muffins
2 cups cubed cooked ham
2 cups chopped cooked fresh asparagus
4 ounces Swiss cheese, shredded
4 eggs, beaten
1/4 cup sour cream

1 1/4 cups milk
2 tablespoons finely chopped white onion
1 tablespoon Dijon mustard
1/8 teaspoon salt
1/8 teaspoon pepper

Grease a 2-quart square baking dish with the butter. Layer one-half of the English muffin pieces, the ham, asparagus, cheese and remaining English muffin pieces in the prepared baking dish. Whisk the eggs and sour cream in a bowl. Stir in the milk, onion, Dijon mustard, salt and pepper. Pour over the layers. Chill, covered, for 2 to 24 hours. Bake, uncovered, in a preheated 325-degree oven for 60 to 65 minutes or to 170 degrees. Let stand for 10 minutes before serving.

Serves 6

Huevos Estrada

1 1/2 pounds ham, chopped
2 onions, chopped
2 ribs celery, chopped
1 tablespoon butter
8 slices bread, toasted, buttered and cubed
16 ounces sharp Cheddar cheese, shredded

12 eggs, beaten
1/2 teaspoon dry mustard
1 1/2 teaspoons salt
4 cups milk
Dash of Tabasco sauce

Sauté the ham, onions and celery in the butter in a nonstick skillet until the vegetables are soft. Combine with the bread, cheese, eggs, dry mustard, salt, milk and Tabasco sauce in a large bowl and mix well. Pour into a 9×13-inch baking dish. Chill for 8 to 10 hours. Bake in a preheated 350-degree oven for 1 1/4 to 1 1/2 hours or until set.

Serves 8 to 10

Country Breakfast Bake

1/4 cup chopped green onions with tops
1/4 cup chopped red bell pepper
3 cups frozen hash brown potatoes
4 slices bacon, crisp-cooked and crumbled
3 tablespoons vegetable oil
4 eggs
Salt and pepper to taste
3/4 cup (3 ounces) shredded
Colby Monterey Jack cheese blend

Combine the green onions, bell pepper, potatoes, bacon and oil in a bowl and mix well. Spread evenly in a 9×9-inch baking dish. Bake in a preheated 450-degree oven for 20 minutes, stirring after 10 minutes. Reduce the oven temperature to 325 degrees. Remove the baking dish from the oven. Make four indentations in the potato mixture with a spoon. Break an egg into each indentation. Sprinkle with salt and pepper. Bake for 15 minutes or until the eggs are set. Remove from the oven. Sprinkle the top evenly with the cheese.

Serves 4

TRUEHEART-ADRIANCE BUILDING

The Junior League of Galveston County, Inc., purchased the Trueheart-Adriance Building in 1967 as a headquarters for the organization. The historic Strand building was designed by Nicholas Clayton and housed the first realty firm in Texas. The building is utilized for meetings, parties, and during the holiday season, JLGC volunteers conduct tours for Galveston's annual Dickens on The Strand. It has seen several facelifts over the years and in 2009 was completely renovated due to damage caused by Hurricane Ike.

Something Old—Something New

A Menu for a
Wedding Shower

Appetizer
Dilled Deviled Eggs 37

Salad
Crab Meat Salad with Avocado 70

Entrées
Ham Asparagus Strata 28
Spicy Cheese Sandwiches 20

Side Dishes
Cheesy Grits Soufflé 27
Zucchini Bake 157

Desserts
Chocolate Chunk Pecan Bars 184
Lollipop Cookies 187

Tantalizing Tidbits

APPETIZERS

It's no secret—Galveston County knows how to throw a party. Whether we are dancing at the Kemah Jazz Festival, eating our weight in blue crabs at the Bolivar Crab Festival, dressing in our Victorian best for Dickens on the Strand, or throwing beads at Mardi Gras, we are always up for a good soiree.

Our calendars are always full around here, as we aren't particular about needing a reason to get together. A party can be thrown on any given day celebrating anything from a football game to someone's birthday, to food and wine. When a hurricane is on the horizon, well, that's all the more reason to gather.

Hosting events is in our blood, and down by the Gulf we do it in style. We know to start a festivity, you need great appetizers to set the scene. These Tantalizing Tidbits will no doubt have your guests sticking around to see what other fun is in store. Grab your beads and put on your dancing shoes…the party is getting started.

The Spot's Shrimp Ceviche

2 pounds fresh medium shrimp
1 small package shrimp boil
2 pounds tomatoes, finely chopped
3 large white onions, finely chopped
2 jalapeño chiles, seeded and
finely chopped

3 tablespoons cilantro
1¼ cups ketchup
2 tablespoons lemon juice
2 tablespoons hot pepper sauce
Salt and pepper to taste

Boil the shrimp with the shrimp boil using the package directions. Drain and let stand until cool. Peel and chop the shrimp. Combine the shrimp, tomatoes, onions, jalapeño chiles annd cilantro in a large bowl and mix well. Mix the ketchup, lemon juice and hot sauce in a bowl. Pour over the shrimp mixture and mix well. Sprinkle with salt and pepper. Chill for 1 to 2 hours before serving. Serve with tortilla chips.

Serves 10 to 12

Southern Shrimp Rémoulade

1½ cups mayonnaise
½ cup Creole mustard
⅓ cup chili sauce or ketchup
½ cup minced onion
2 tablespoons lemon juice
1 tablespoon Worcestershire sauce
2 teaspoons horseradish

1 teaspoon chopped garlic
1 teaspoon white pepper
½ teaspoon celery seeds
1½ pounds cooked shrimp, peeled
and chilled
1 head green leaf lettuce, rinsed
and torn

Combine the mayonnaise, Creole mustard, chili sauce, onion, lemon juice, Worcestershire sauce, horseradish, garlic, white pepper and celery seeds in a bowl and mix well. Chill for 2 to 10 hours. Pour over the shrimp in a bowl just before serving and toss to coat. Spoon over a bed of lettuce leaves on individual serving plates or in martini glasses. Garnish with capers and lemon slices.

Serves 6

Cajun Crab Fritters with Creole Sauce

Creole Sauce

1/2 cup Creole mustard

1/4 cup mayonnaise

1 teaspoon lemon juice

1/2 teaspoon hot pepper sauce

1/4 teaspoon pepper

Cajun Crab Fritters

8 ounces fresh crab meat

1 cup baking mix

3/4 teaspoon salt

1/8 teaspoon garlic powder

1/2 teaspoon ground red pepper

1 tablespoon chopped fresh parsley

1/2 teaspoon grated lemon zest

1/4 cup milk

1 egg

2 tablespoons fresh lemon juice

1/4 teaspoon Worcestershire sauce

Vegetable oil for frying

To prepare the sauce, blend the Creole mustard, mayonnaise, lemon juice, hot sauce and pepper in a small bowl. Chill until serving time.

To prepare the fritters, drain and flake the crab meat, removing any bits of shell. Mix the baking mix, salt, garlic powder, red pepper, parsley and lemon zest in a bowl and make a well in the center. Combine the milk, egg, lemon juice and Worcestershire sauce in a bowl and mix well. Add to the well in the flour mixture and stir just until moistened. Stir in the crab meat. Pour oil into a Dutch oven to a depth of 2 inches. Heat the oil to 375 degrees. Drop the batter by teaspoonfuls into the hot oil. Deep-fry for 30 seconds or until golden brown. Drain on paper towels. Serve with the sauce.

Makes 10 fritters

HARVEST MOON REGATTA

The Harvest Moon Regatta is an annual sailboat race that takes place in October. Its distinct timing is chosen on the day that has the fullest and brightest moon, which is considered the harvest moon. Contestants begin sailing this weekend-long race from the Galveston jetties onto Port Aransas, and then back to Galveston Island. This racing tradition began in 1987 with only seventeen participants. Now, there are more than 260 sailors that take part in this wonderful tradition.

Crab Deviled Eggs

12 hard-cooked eggs
8 ounces fresh lump crab meat, cleaned
1/4 cup mayonnaise
1 tablespoon Dijon mustard
1 tablespoon minced capers
2 tablespoons caper juice
1 teaspoon minced garlic
1/8 teaspoon salt, or to taste
1/8 teaspoon pepper, or to taste

Peel the eggs and cut into halves lengthwise. Mash the egg yolks in a medium bowl. Add the crab meat, mayonnaise, Dijon mustard, capers, caper juice and garlic and mix well. Season with the salt and pepper. Spoon or pipe the mixture into the egg whites. Chill, covered, to allow the flavors to blend.

Serves 12

Martini Deviled Eggs

6 hard-cooked eggs

1/4 cup good-quality mayonnaise

1 1/2 teaspoons vodka

1 1/2 tablespoons green olive juice

1/4 teaspoon cayenne pepper

1 1/2 teaspoons finely chopped flat-leaf parsley

Salt and black pepper to taste

Peel the eggs and cut into halves lengthwise. Mash the egg yolks in a medium bowl. Add the mayonnaise, vodka, olive juice, cayenne pepper, parsley, salt and black pepper and mix well. Spoon or pipe into the egg whites. Garnish with sliced green olives.

Serves 12

Dill Deviled Eggs

1/2 cup shredded cucumber

1 teaspoon salt

6 hard-cooked eggs

1/4 cup sour cream

1/4 teaspoon dill weed

1/8 teaspoon pepper

1/8 teaspoon salt

Toss the cucumber and 1 teaspoon salt in a bowl. Let stand for 15 minutes. Drain well, pressing out the excess liquid. Peel the eggs and cut into halves lengthwise. Mash the egg yolks in a medium bowl. Add the sour cream, dill weed, pepper and 1/8 teaspoon salt and mix well. Stir in the drained cucumber. Spoon 1 heaping tablespoon of the cucumber mixture into each egg white. Chill, covered, to allow the flavors to blend.

Serves 6

Bacon-Wrapped Asparagus Bundles

¹/₂ cup mayonnaise

2 teaspoons Sriracha sauce

2 tablespoons plus 1 teaspoon fresh lime juice

1¹/₂ tablespoons finely chopped cilantro

¹/₂ teaspoon salt

Pepper to taste

30 medium asparagus spears, trimmed

10 slices peppered bacon

¹/₄ cup extra-virgin olive oil

³/₄ teaspoon salt

*W*hisk the mayonnaise, Sriracha sauce, lime juice, cilantro, ¹/₂ teaspoon salt and pepper in a small bowl. Chill in an airtight container until serving time or up to 1 week.

Separate the asparagus spears into bundles of three spears each. Wrap a slice of bacon carefully around each bundle, beginning at about ¹/₂ inch from the bottom of the tip and securing with wooden picks. Place on a rimmed baking sheet. Drizzle with the olive oil. Sprinkle with ³/₄ teaspoon salt and pepper. Roast in a preheated 450-degree oven for 20 to 22 minutes or until the asparagus begins to wilt and the bacon begins to brown, turning halfway through. Remove to a serving platter and discard the wooden picks. Serve with the sauce.

Serves 10

Soy Bourbon Chicken

1/2 cup soy sauce

1/2 cup packed brown sugar

1/2 teaspoon garlic powder

1 teaspoon ginger

2 tablespoons dried minced onion

1/2 cup bourbon

2 tablespoons white wine

1 pound chicken thighs, cut into large
   bite-size pieces

Mix the soy sauce, brown sugar, garlic powder, ginger, dried onion and bourbon in a bowl. Pour over the chicken in a bowl. Marinate, covered, in the refrigerator for 3 to 10 hours, stirring frequently. Drain the chicken, reserving the marinade. Place the chicken in a single layer in a baking dish. Bake in a preheated 350-degree oven for 1 hour, basting with the reserved marinade every 10 minutes. Remove the chicken to a bowl. Scrape the pan juices with all of the brown bits into a skillet. Cook until heated through. Stir in the wine. Add the chicken. Cook for 1 minute and serve.

Serves 8

Chicken Zuengenfuss

4 chicken breasts

1 cup chopped celery

1 cup water

8 ounces cream cheese, softened

1/4 cup (1/2 stick) butter, softened

2 bunches scallions, chopped

2 (8-count) cans crescent rolls

1/4 cup (1/2 stick) butter, melted

2 cups chopped walnuts

1 (10-ounce) can cream of chicken soup

1 teaspoon sage

Cook the chicken with the celery in the water in a saucepan until cooked through; drain, reserving the broth. Cut the chicken into bite-size pieces, discarding the skin and bones. Mix the cream cheese, 1/4 cup butter and the scallions in a bowl. Unroll the crescent roll dough. Press two of the triangles together to form a rectangle. Place a spoonful of the cream cheese mixture, some of the celery and some of the chicken in the center of the rectangle. Fold up the edges and pinch together to form a pouch. Brush with some of the melted butter and roll in the walnuts. Place in a baking dish. Repeat to form eight pouches. Bake in a preheated 350-degree oven for 15 to 25 minutes or until golden brown.

Bring the chicken soup, reserved broth and sage to a boil in a saucepan. Pour over the chicken pouches and serve.

Serves 8

One-Bite Cheese Truffles

4 ounces cream cheese, softened
1/2 teaspoon Worcestershire sauce
1/4 teaspoon coarsely ground pepper
2 teaspoons finely chopped green onions
4 ounces crumbled Gorgonzola cheese
1/2 cup crumbled cooked bacon

Beat the cream cheese, Worcestershire sauce, pepper, green onions and Gorgonzola cheese at medium speed in a mixing bowl until creamy. Chill, tightly covered, for 1 hour or until firm. The cheese mixture may be chilled for up to 3 days. Shape the cheese mixture into 3/4-inch balls. Roll in the bacon. Serve immediately or chill, covered, until serving time. Let stand at room temperature for 30 minutes before serving. Serve with apple slices, pear slices and grapes.

Substitute goat cheese for the Gorgonzola cheese and roll in chopped toasted pecans. Serve with dried figs and apricots.

Substitute feta cheese for the Gorgonzola cheese and chopped fresh parsley for the bacon. Serve with cucumber slices, whole almonds, grape tomatoes and kalamata olives.

Serves 6

Artichoke Croustades

18 slices soft white bread, crusts trimmed
3 tablespoons butter, melted
1 (6-ounce) jar artichoke hearts, drained and chopped
3 tablespoons mayonnaise
1 tablespoon chopped green onions
3 tablespoons grated Parmesan cheese
1/4 teaspoon freshly ground pepper
1/4 teaspoon salt
1 tablespoon chopped green onions
1 tablespoon grated Parmesan cheese

Roll the bread slices with a rolling pin to flatten. Brush with the butter. Fit into lightly greased small muffin cups. Bake in a preheated 350-degree oven for 12 minutes or until the edges are light brown. Combine the artichoke hearts, mayonnaise, 1 tablespoon green onions and 3 tablespoons Parmesan cheese in a bowl and mix well. Spoon into the croustades. Broil 6 inches from the heat source until the filling is bubbly. Sprinkle with 1 tablespoon green onions and 1 tablespoon Parmesan cheese. Jumbo muffin cups can be used, but the artichoke filling will need to be doubled.

Serves 18

Dickens on the Strand began thirty-five years ago by Galvestonians and the Galveston Historic Foundation to celebrate and restore the Strand's historic buildings and their significance. This annual festival takes place along the Strand during the first weekend of December. Dickens will take you and your family on an enchanted journey through the history of a bustling nineteenth-century Victorian city. The event includes costumed street vendors, bagpipers, parades, strolling carolers, food, and re-enactments of A Christmas Carol.

Sicilian Stuffed Mushrooms

20 large fresh mushrooms
8 ounces sweet Italian turkey sausage, casings removed
1 garlic clove, minced
1 tablespoon extra-virgin olive oil
2 tablespoons finely chopped parsley
1/4 cup (1 ounce) grated Parmesan cheese
1 teaspoon extra-virgin olive oil
1/8 teaspoon salt
1/8 teaspoon pepper
1/4 cup water
1 tablespoon extra-virgin olive oil

Clean the mushrooms well. Remove the stems, reserving the caps. Chop the stems finely. Brown the sausage with the mushroom stems and garlic in 1 tablespoon olive oil in a skillet, stirring until crumbly. Add the parsley, cheese, 1 teaspoon olive oil, the salt and pepper and mix well. Fill the reserved mushroom caps with the sausage mixture and place in a shallow baking pan. Pour the water and 1 tablespoon olive oil into the bottom of the pan. Bake in a preheated 350-degree oven for 20 minutes.

Serves 4

Spinach Italian Tarts

2 tablespoons chopped white onion
1/2 teaspoon minced garlic
1 teaspoon extra-virgin olive oil
4 ounces Italian pork, turkey or
chicken sausage
1/4 teaspoon salt
1/4 teaspoon pepper
1/4 teaspoon Italian seasoning
1 egg, beaten
2 tablespoons tomato sauce
6 tablespoons crumbled feta cheese
1 (10-ounce) package frozen chopped spinach,
thawed and well drained
2 (15-count) packages miniature phyllo shells

Sauté the onion and garlic in the olive oil in a saucepan for 3 minutes or until tender. Remove from the heat to cool. Remove the casings from the sausage. Brown the sausage with the salt, pepper and Italian seasoning in a skillet over medium heat for 8 to 10 minutes or until the sausage is cooked through, stirring until crumbly. Drain and let stand until cool.

Pulse the onion mixture, sausage, egg, tomato sauce, cheese and spinach in a food processor until blended. Fill the phyllo shells with the sausage mixture and place on a baking sheet. Bake in a preheated 375-degree oven for 10 minutes. Serve warm. These may be prepared in advance, chilled and brought to room temperature before baking.

Serves 15

Basil Tomato Tart

1 refrigerator pie pastry
1 1/2 cups (6 ounces) shredded mozzarella cheese
5 Roma tomatoes or 4 medium tomatoes
1 cup loosely packed fresh basil leaves
4 garlic cloves
1/3 cup grated Parmesan cheese
1/2 cup mayonnaise
1/8 teaspoon white pepper

Line a 9-inch pie plate with the pie pastry, fluting the edge. Bake in a preheated 375-degree oven for 10 minutes. Remove from the oven and sprinkle with 1/2 cup of the mozzarella cheese. Cool on a wire rack. Maintain the oven temperature.

Cut the tomatoes into wedges and drain on paper towels. Arrange over the mozzarella cheese in the prebaked pie shell. Process the basil and garlic in a food processor until coarsely chopped. Sprinkle over the tomatoes. Combine the remaining 1 cup mozzarella cheese, the Parmesan cheese, mayonnaise and white pepper in a bowl and mix well. Spread evenly over the layers. Bake for 35 to 40 minutes or until the top is golden brown and bubbly. Sprinkle with additional basil leaves if desired. Serve warm.

Makes 8 appetizer servings or 4 main dish servings

Salmon Spread

8 ounces cream cheese, softened
1/2 cup mayonnaise
1 tablespoon lemon juice
1 teaspoon horseradish
1 tablespoon chopped green onions

6 ounces smoked salmon, flaked
1 cup (4 ounces) shredded sharp
    Cheddar cheese
1 teaspoon dill weed

Beat the cream cheese, mayonnaise, lemon juice and horseradish in a bowl until creamy. Combine the green onions, salmon, Cheddar cheese and dill weed in a bowl and toss to mix. Stir into the cream cheese mixture. Shape into a log on a serving platter and cover with plastic wrap. Chill for 4 to 6 hours to blend the flavors before serving. Serve with crackers.

Serves 12

Basil Blue Cheesecake

2 cups loosely packed fresh basil
2 cups loosely packed fresh parsley
1 teaspoon minced garlic
16 ounces cream cheese, softened

8 ounces blue cheese, crumbled
2 eggs
2 egg whites

Pulse the basil, parsley and garlic in a food processor until finely chopped. Scrap into a bowl and wipe out the food processor bowl. Process the cream cheese, blue cheese, eggs and egg whites in the food processor until smooth. Stir 1/2 cup of the cheese mixture into the basil mixture. Pour one-half of the remaining cheese mixture into a greased 8-inch springform pan. Drop one-half of the basil cheese mixture on top. Repeat the layers with the remaining ingredients and swirl lightly to marbleize. Bake in a preheated 325-degree oven for 1 hour. The cheesecake will rise and then sink. Remove from the oven to cool. The top will crack as it cools. Cover tightly with plastic wrap and chill until serving time. Release the side of the springform pan. Serve cold with crackers.

Serves 12 to 15

Garlic Feta Cheese Spread

1 garlic clove, crushed
1/2 teaspoon salt
8 ounces feta cheese, crumbled
12 ounces cream cheese, cut into cubes and softened
1/2 cup mayonnaise
1/4 teaspoon dried dill weed
1/4 teaspoon dried basil
1/4 teaspoon dried thyme
1/4 teaspoon dried marjoram

Mix the garlic and salt in a bowl. Process the garlic mixture, feta cheese, cream cheese, mayonnaise, dill weed, basil, thyme and marjoram in a food processor until blended. Spoon into a serving bowl. Chill, covered, for 2 hours before serving. Serve with crudités, toast points or French bread. The spread may be stored in the refrigerator for up to 1 week.

Serves 6

Crab Meat Guacamole

3 ripe avocados, mashed
2 tablespoons mayonnaise
1 teaspoon lemon juice
1/2 tablespoon grated onion
1/2 teaspoon hot pepper sauce
Creole Seasoning to taste
1 tablespoon diced tomato
1 pound fresh white crab meat,
shells removed and meat flaked

Combine the avocados, mayonnaise, lemon juice, onion, hot sauce and Creole seasoning in a medium bowl and mix well. Fold in the crab meat and serve.

Serves 6

Hot Jalapeño Crab Meat Dip

1 pound lump crab meat or imitation crab meat, shells removed
1 teaspoon chopped garlic
1/2 cup chopped pickled jalapeño chiles
4 ounces Pepper Jack cheese, shredded
1 teaspoon Worcestershire sauce
1 teaspoon hot pepper sauce
1/2 teaspoon salt
1/2 cup mayonnaise or reduced-fat mayonnaise
2 ounces Parmigiano-Reggiano cheese, grated

Combine the crab meat, garlic, jalapeño chiles, Pepper Jack cheese, Worcestershire sauce, hot sauce, salt and mayonnaise in a medium bowl and toss gently to mix. Spoon into a shallow medium baking dish. Sprinkle the Parmigiano-Reggiano cheese evenly over the top. Bake in a preheated 350-degree oven for 25 minutes or until golden brown and bubbly. Remove from the oven and let stand for 5 minutes. Serve with melba toast.

Serves 6 to 8

Seabrook Shrimp Dip

8 ounces cream cheese, softened
1/2 cup sour cream
2 tablespoons mayonnaise
2 teaspoons Worcestershire sauce
2 teaspoons finely chopped green onions
1 teaspoon garlic salt or garlic powder
1 teaspoon seasoned salt
2 teaspoons lemon juice
2 pounds or more fresh shrimp, cooked, peeled and chopped

Combine the cream cheese, sour cream, mayonnaise, Worcestershire sauce, green onions, garlic salt, seasoned salt and lemon juice in a bowl and mix well. Stir in the shrimp. Serve with chips or crackers.

Serves 7 or 8

Seafood Artichoke Dip

1 cup (4 ounces) shredded
Cheddar cheese
1 cup (4 ounces) grated Parmesan cheese
1 (14-ounce) can artichoke hearts,
drained and chopped
1/2 cup chopped green onions

1/2 teaspoon garlic salt
1/2 cup mayonnaise
1 1/2 cups coarsely chopped peeled
cooked shrimp (optional)
1 1/2 cups fresh lump crab meat

Combine the Cheddar cheese, Parmesan cheese, artichoke hearts, green onions, garlic salt and mayonnaise in a bowl and mix well. Stir in the shrimp and crab meat. Spoon into a 9-inch baking dish. Bake in a preheated 350-degree oven for 20 minutes or until bubbly and light brown.

Serves 10 to 20

Creamy Bacon Blue Cheese Dip

7 slices bacon, chopped
2 garlic cloves, minced
8 ounces cream cheese, softened
1/4 cup half-and-half

1 1/4 cups crumbled blue cheese
2 tablespoons chopped chives
3 tablespoons chopped smoked almonds

Cook the bacon in a large skillet over medium-high heat for 7 minutes or until almost crisp; drain. Add the garlic. Cook for 3 minutes or until the bacon is crisp. Beat the cream cheese in a bowl until smooth. Add the half-and-half and mix well. Stir in the bacon mixture, blue cheese and chives. Spoon into a 2-cup ovenproof serving dish. Bake, covered with foil, in a preheated 350-degree oven for 30 minutes or until heated through. Sprinkle with the almonds. Serve with sliced Granny Smith apples or French bread. The dip may be prepared 1 day in advance and chilled or frozen. Bring to room temperature before baking.

Serves 4 to 6

Pan-Fried Onion Dip

2 large yellow onions

¼ cup (½ stick) unsalted butter

¼ cup olive oil

¼ teaspoon cayenne pepper

1 teaspoon kosher salt

½ teaspoon freshly ground black pepper

4 ounces cream cheese, softened

½ cup sour cream

½ cup good-quality mayonnaise

Cut the onions into halves. Cut each half into slices ⅛ inch thick. Heat the butter and olive oil in a large sauté pan over medium heat. Add the onions, cayenne pepper, kosher salt and black pepper. Sauté for 10 minutes. Reduce the heat to medium-low. Cook for 30 minutes or until the onions are brown and caramelized, stirring occasionally. Remove from the heat to cool. Beat the cream cheese, sour cream and mayonnaise in a mixing bowl until smooth. Add the onions and mix well. Adjust the seasonings to taste. Serve at room temperature with thick kettle-cooked potato chips, crackers or fresh vegetables.

Serves 10 to 20

Shrimp Salsa

3 pounds fresh shrimp, steamed, peeled, deveined and chopped

3 large avocados, chopped

8 small Roma tomatoes, seeded and chopped

½ large red onion, finely chopped

2 to 4 jalapeño chiles, seeded and chopped

1 cup cilantro, chopped

Juice of 2 limes

1 (12-ounce) jar cocktail sauce

¼ cup ketchup

Salt to taste

Combine the shrimp, avocados, tomatoes, red onion, jalapeño chiles, cilantro and lime juice in a bowl and mix gently. Stir in the cocktail sauce, ketchup and salt. Chill, covered, for 1 hour. Serve with tortilla chips. For a hotter salsa, do not seed the jalapeño chiles.

Serves 30 to 35

Texas Caviar

2 (15-ounce) cans black-eyed peas, drained and rinsed
2 avocados, chopped
1/2 red onion, chopped
1 bell pepper, chopped
1 or 2 jalapeño chiles, seeded and chopped
1 small can chopped black olives
1 (10-ounce) can tomatoes with green chiles
1/3 cup Italian salad dressing
1/2 cup fresh lime juice
Salt to taste

Combine the peas, avocados, red onion, bell pepper, jalapeño chiles, black olives, tomatoes with green chiles, salad dressing, lime juice and salt in a large bowl and mix well. Serve with tortilla chips.

Serves 8 to 10

Any Given Sunday

A Menu for a Super Bowl Party

Appetizers
Creamy Bacon Blue Cheese Dip 49
Hot Jalapeño Crab Meat Dip 48

Salad
Black Bean Salad 65

Bread
Jalapeño Muffins 74

Entrées
Cheesy Chicken Chili 95
Garlic Mustard Beef Skewers 109

Desserts
Lemon Bars 185
Cream Cheese Bars 185

Light and Breezy
SOUPS, SALADS, BREADS

Not only is Galveston County loaded with culinary delights, it is also home to places that tickle the inner artist in us. From the Harbour Playhouse in Dickinson, which boasts a crew of volunteer actors, to the 1894 Grand Opera House, a historic landmark in Galveston, lovers of the stage can find it here.

If shopping is what you crave, look no further. The Historic Strand District, originally known as the "Wall Street of the Southwest," is in the heart of downtown Galveston and is home to souvenir shops, trendy boutiques, sweet candy stores, and famous ice cream parlors. Postoffice Street, which looks like it was painted by Van Gogh himself, also boasts many antique shops, art galleries, and restaurants. If you're lucky, Art Walk will be in full swing, and you will have the chance to hear local music and see local artists at their best.

Have something "Light and Breezy," and then take a stroll with us around historic Galveston.

Mario's Seawall Italian Restaurant
sponsor

Oyster Rockefeller Soup

1 1/2 cups chicken broth

1 small onion, finely chopped

1 rib celery, finely chopped

2 garlic cloves, minced

1 cup chopped fresh spinach

1 pint shucked oysters

1/3 cup grated Parmesan cheese

2 cups half-and-half

2 tablespoons cornstarch

1 1/2 teaspoons anise seeds

1/2 teaspoon salt

1/8 teaspoon pepper

Cook the broth, onion, celery and garlic in a large saucepan for 5 minutes. Add the spinach. Simmer for 5 minutes. Drain the oysters, reserving the liquor. Add the reserved oyster liquor to the spinach mixture. Continue to simmer, stirring occasionally. Stir in the cheese. Combine the half-and-half, cornstarch, anise seeds, salt and pepper in a bowl. Add to the simmering soup gradually, stirring constantly. Cook until the soup is thickened and bubbly, stirring constantly. Stir in the oysters. Cook until the edges of the oysters curl. Ladle into soup bowls and serve immediately.

Serves 6

Chicken and Shrimp Tortilla Soup

1 1/2 cups chopped cooked chicken breasts

2 tablespoons vegetable oil

1 large onion, chopped

6 ounces frozen or fresh baby shrimp

1 teaspoon ground cumin

4 cups chicken broth

1 (10-ounce) can tomatoes with
green chiles

3 tablespoons chopped fresh cilantro

2 tablespoons lime juice

Sauté the chicken in the oil in a heavy saucepan until cooked through. Add the onion and sauté until the onion is tender. Stir in the shrimp. Cook for 3 minutes or until the shrimp turn pink. Stir in the cumin, broth and tomatoes with green chiles. Bring to a slow boil. Remove from the heat. Add the cilantro and lime juice just before serving. Ladle into soup bowls. Garnish with shredded Monterey Jack cheese and sliced avocado. Serve with tortilla chips.

Serves 4 to 6

Louisiana Shrimp and Corn Chowder

12 cups (3 quarts) chicken stock

5 large white onions, chopped

3/4 cup (1 1/2 sticks) butter

3/4 cup plus 2 tablespoons all-purpose flour

3 pounds frozen corn kernels

2 tablespoons finely chopped garlic

3 bay leaves

6 tablespoons chopped parsley

2 teaspoons paprika

2 teaspoons hot pepper sauce

Salt and pepper to taste

6 cups (1/4-inch) cubes peeled yellow potatoes

2 carrots, peeled and finely chopped

3 pounds shrimp, peeled

3 cups half-and-half

Heat the stock in a large stockpot. Sauté the onions in the butter in a large stockpot over medium heat for 15 minutes or until translucent. Add the flour a small amount at a time, stirring constantly. Cook until thickened, stirring constantly. Add about 4 cups of the hot stock, stirring constantly until smooth. Stir in the remaining stock gradually. Cook for a few more minutes or until the mixture begins to thicken, stirring constantly.

Add the corn, garlic, bay leaves, parsley, paprika, hot sauce, salt and pepper. Cook until the corn is tender. Add the potatoes and carrots. Cook for 35 to 45 minutes or until the potatoes are tender. Adjust the seasonings to taste. Discard the bay leaves. Mash the potatoes slightly with a potato masher if needed. Add the shrimp. Cook until the shrimp turn pink. Stir in the half-and-half. Do not boil. Adjust the seasonings to taste. Ladle into soup bowls. Garnish with crumbled bacon and chopped green onions.

Serves 12

Chipotle Chicken Soup

1 tablespoon olive oil
1 chipotle chile in adobo sauce, finely chopped
2 cups chopped onions
1 cup chopped carrots
1/2 cup chopped celery
1 teaspoon ground cumin
1/2 teaspoon dried oregano
1/2 teaspoon dried thyme
6 garlic cloves, crushed
6 cups fat-free chicken broth

1 1/2 pounds boneless skinless chicken breasts
2 red potatoes, cut into 1/2-inch pieces
1 (15-ounce) can white or golden hominy, drained and rinsed
1/4 cup whipping cream
1 teaspoon adobo sauce
1 cup chopped seeded plum tomatoes
1/4 cup chopped fresh cilantro
1/2 teaspoon salt

Heat the olive oil in a large Dutch oven over medium heat. Add the chipotle chile, onions, carrots, celery, cumin, oregano, thyme and garlic. Cook for 7 minutes or until the onion is tender, stirring frequently. Stir in the broth and bring to a boil. Add the chicken. Cover and reduce the heat to medium-low. Simmer for 30 minutes or until the chicken is tender and cooked through.

Remove the chicken with a slotted spoon and cool slightly. Shred the chicken with two forks. Cover and keep warm. Remove the pan from the heat. Let stand for 5 minutes. Purée the broth mixture in three batches in a blender. Return the puréed broth mixture to the pan. Stir in the potatoes and hominy. Bring to a simmer over medium heat. Cook, uncovered, for 20 minutes or until the potatoes are tender. Stir in the chicken and whipping cream. Simmer for 5 minutes. Remove from the heat. Stir in the adobo sauce, tomatoes, cilantro and salt. Ladle into soup bowls. Serve with lime wedges.

Serves 8

Black Bean Soup

1 pound dried black beans
2 tablespoons extra-virgin olive oil
1 onion, chopped
1 carrot, chopped
2 garlic cloves, minced
2 bay leaves
2 teaspoons dried oregano
1 teaspoon minced jalapeño chile
1 pound bacon
9 cups (or more) water
2 teaspoons kosher salt, or to taste
1/4 cup sherry
1 teaspoon balsamic vinegar
2 teaspoons ground pepper, or to taste
1 bunch scallions, chopped

Sort and rinse the beans. Place in a large saucepan and cover the beans with 2 inches of cold water. Bring to a boil. Cook for 5 minutes. Remove from the heat. Cover and set aside for 1 hour. Drain the beans.

Heat the olive oil in a large stockpot over medium to medium-high heat. Add the onion and carrot. Cook for 10 minutes or until light brown. Add the beans, garlic, bay leaves, oregano, jalapeño chile and bacon to the stockpot. Add 9 cups water and bring to a full rolling boil. Add 2 teaspoons salt. Reduce the heat to a simmer. Simmer for 1 1/2 hours or until the beans and bacon are tender. Remove from the heat and cool slightly. Remove the bacon and set aside. Discard the bay leaves.

Purée the soup with an immersion blender or in batches in a blender, adding additional water if needed for the desired consistency. Add the sherry and vinegar and mix well. Return the soup to medium heat and stir in the reserved bacon. Bring to a simmer. Season with salt to taste and the pepper. Ladle into warm soup bowls and top with the scallions.

Serves 8

Fennel Apple Bisque

1 1/2 pounds fennel with stalks
2 tablespoons butter
1 large white onion, chopped
4 cups (or more) chicken broth
2 large Fuji apples, peeled and chopped

2 teaspoons salt
2 teaspoons pepper
1 cup fresh watercress leaves
1/2 cup crumbled blue cheese

Trim the root end and stalks from the fennel bulb. Reserve some of the feathery fronds for garnish. Chop the fennel bulb. Heat the butter in a saucepan over medium to high heat. Add the onion and sauté for 5 minutes or until softened. Add the fennel, broth, apples, salt and pepper. Bring to a boil; reduce the heat. Simmer for 15 to 20 minutes or until the fennel is soft. Stir in the watercress. Cook until wilted. Purée the soup in batches. Return to the saucepan and reheat, adding additional broth if needed for the desired consistency. Ladle into soup bowls and top with the blue cheese. Garnish with the reserved fennel fronds.

Serves 4 to 6

Roasted Red Pepper Soup

3 large red bell peppers
2 tablespoons olive oil
1 large yellow onion, chopped
3 Yukon gold potatoes, peeled and coarsely chopped

2 teaspoons salt
2 teaspoons pepper
4 cups (or more) chicken broth

Broil the bell peppers on a baking sheet for 10 to 12 minutes or until completely charred. Remove from the oven to cool. Peel the bell peppers, discarding the stems and seeds. Chop the bell peppers coarsely. Heat the olive oil in a stockpot over medium-high heat. Add the onion and sauté until light brown. Add the bell peppers, potatoes, salt, pepper and broth. Bring to a boil; reduce the heat. Simmer, covered, for 10 to 15 minutes or until the potatoes are tender. Purée the soup in batches and return to the stockpot, adding additional broth if needed for the desired consistency. Ladle into soup bowls.

Serves 4 to 6

Cornucopia Salad

Glazed Almonds
1/2 cup sliced almonds
3 tablespoons sugar

Cornucopia Salad Dressing
1/4 cup canola oil
1 teaspoon salt
1/2 teaspoon pepper
2 tablespoons sugar
3 tablespoons red wine vinegar
Dash of Tabasco sauce

Salad
1 head romaine or baby spinach, torn
1 cup chopped celery
1 avocado, chopped
1 green apple, chopped
1/3 cup orange-flavored dried cranberries
1/2 cup crumbled blue cheese or feta cheese
1 (11-ounce) can mandarin oranges, drained

To prepare the almonds, sauté the almonds with the sugar in a hot skillet over medium heat until the almonds are brown. Remove from the skillet to cool.

To prepare the dressing, whisk the oil, salt, pepper, sugar, vinegar and Tabasco sauce in a bowl until blended.

To prepare the salad, combine the lettuce, celery, avocado, apple, dried cranberries, cheese and mandarin oranges in a salad bowl. Add the dressing and toss to coat. Sprinkle with the almonds.

Serves 4 to 6

Roquefort Pear Salad

Mustard Vinaigrette
1/3 cup olive oil
3 tablespoons red wine vinegar
1 1/2 teaspoons sugar
1 1/2 teaspoons Dijon mustard
1 garlic clove, chopped
1/2 teaspoon salt
1/2 teaspoon pepper

Salad
1/2 cup pecans
1/4 cup sugar
1 head green leafy lettuce, torn into bite-size pieces
3 pears, peeled and chopped
5 ounces Roquefort cheese, crumbled
1 large avocado, chopped
1/2 cup thinly sliced green onions

To prepare the vinaigrette, whisk the olive oil, vinegar, sugar, Dijon mustard, garlic, salt and pepper in a bowl until blended.

To prepare the salad, sauté the pecans with the sugar in a skillet over medium heat until the sugar melts and the pecans are caramelized. Remove carefully to a plate to cool. Break into pieces. Layer the lettuce, pears, cheese, avocado and green onions in a large salad bowl. Pour the vinaigrette over the salad. Sprinkle with the pecans and serve.

Serves 6

The Galveston Art Walk is an event that takes place on Saturdays every six to eight weeks on Strand and Postoffice streets in Galveston. It highlights Galveston's visual and performing arts and is organized by the Galveston Arts Center. Art galleries, retail shops, and restaurants stay open late and feature local, national, and internationally recognized artists. Guests stroll through the heart of Galveston's historical district and are welcomed with complimentary wine and cheese.

Spiced Orange Spinach Salad

3 tablespoons vegetable oil

3 tablespoons rice vinegar

2 teaspoons honey

2 teaspoons minced ginger

1 teaspoon Dijon mustard

1/4 teaspoon sesame oil

Salt and pepper to taste

Salad

8 cups baby spinach

1/4 cucumber, seeded and thinly sliced

1/2 cup sliced almonds, toasted

1/2 cup sliced mushrooms

1 (11-ounce) can mandarin oranges, drained

1/4 cup sliced scallions

1/2 cup chow mein noodles

To prepare the dressing, whisk the vegetable oil, vinegar, honey, ginger, Dijon mustard, sesame oil, salt and pepper in a bowl until blended.

To prepare the salad, combine the spinach, cucumber, almonds, mushrooms, mandarin oranges, scallions and chow mein noodles in a large salad bowl. Add the dressing and toss to coat.

Serves 4

Postoffice Street is part of the Strand

National Historic Landmark District

in Galveston, which is located

between 19th and 25th Streets.

The area is known as the "Arts and

Entertainment District" because of

the many art galleries, restaurants,

and antique shops that are located

along its path. This street is also

home to many festivals including

Art Walk, Kid's Fest, ARToberFest,

and the Fat Tuesday Block Party.

The 1894 Opera House also sits

along Postoffice.

Caesar Salad

2 ounces pine nuts
6 ounces romaine, torn into bite-size pieces
1 large egg
3 tablespoons fresh lemon juice
2 tablespoons anchovy paste
1 tablespoon minced garlic
1/2 tablespoon Worcestershire sauce
1/3 cup olive oil
1/4 teaspoon salt
1/4 teaspoon pepper
1 cup (4 ounces) grated Parmesan cheese

Toast the pine nuts in a skillet until brown. Place the lettuce in a salad bowl and add the pine nuts. Process the egg, lemon juice, anchovy paste, garlic, Worcestershire sauce, olive oil, salt, pepper and cheese in a blender until blended. Pour over the lettuce mixture and toss to coat. Serve with additional Parmesan cheese if desired.

If you are concerned about using raw eggs, use eggs pasteurized in their shells, which are sold at some specialty food stores.

Serves 4

Nut and Berry Coleslaw

10 cups chopped shredded cabbage
1 red bell pepper, chopped
1 (6-ounce) package dried cranberries
1/2 cup chopped green onions
4 ounces sliced or slivered almonds,
lightly toasted

1/2 cup sour cream
1/2 cup spicy mustard
1 tablespoon Worcestershire sauce
1 tablespoon finely chopped garlic
2 avocados, chopped

Combine the cabbage, bell pepper, cranberries, green onions and almonds in a large bowl and mix well. Blend the sour cream, mustard, Worcestershire sauce and garlic in a small bowl. Stir in the avocados. Add to the cabbage mixture and stir gently to coat. Store in an airtight container in the refrigerator until serving time. Serve cold.

Serves 15

Black Bean Salad

1 (15-ounce) can black beans, drained
and rinsed, or 1 1/2 cups cooked
dried black beans
1 (15-ounce) can whole kernel
corn, drained
1/2 cup chopped green onions or shallots
2 jalapeño chiles, seeded and minced, or
1 bell pepper, minced

2 large tomatoes, chopped
2 avocados, cut into chunks
1/2 cup fresh cilantro, chopped
1/4 cup fresh basil, chopped
2 tablespoons lime juice
1 tablespoon olive oil
1/2 to 1 teaspoon sugar, or to taste
Salt and pepper to taste

Combine the beans, corn, green onions, jalapeño chiles, tomatoes, avocados, cilantro, basil, lime juice and olive oil in a large bowl and mix well. Add the sugar, salt and pepper. The sugar will help balance the acidity from the tomatoes and lime juice. Chill, covered, until serving time. You may also serve this as a dip with tortilla chips.

Serves 8 to 10

Fresh Tomato and Mozzarella Salad

2 tablespoons red wine vinegar
2 teaspoons olive oil
1 teaspoon Dijon mustard
Salt and pepper to taste
2 cups cherry tomato or grape tomato halves
1 cup chopped fresh mozzarella cheese
2 tablespoons thinly sliced fresh basil

Whisk the vinegar, olive oil, Dijon mustard, salt and pepper in a bowl until blended. Add the tomatoes, mozzarella cheese and basil and toss to coat.

Serves 2

Potato and Corn Summer Salad

1 1/2 pounds small red potatoes
2 cups cooked fresh corn from the cob
1/2 cup each chopped red onion, celery and cucumber
1/3 cup vegetable oil
3 tablespoons cider vinegar
1/2 teaspoon salt
1/4 teaspoon pepper
1/2 teaspoon chopped fresh thyme
1 tablespoon chopped parsley

Place the potatoes in a large saucepan and cover with cold water. Bring to a boil. Reduce the heat to low and simmer for 15 minutes or until tender; drain. Cut the potatoes into halves or quarters. Mix the potatoes, corn, onion, celery and cucumber in a large bowl. Combine the oil, vinegar, salt, pepper and thyme in a jar with a tight-fitting lid. Seal the jar and shake well. Pour over the potato mixture and stir to coat. Stir in the parsley.

Serves 6 to 8

Momo's Potato Salad

5 to 7 pounds white California potatoes
1 rib celery, finely chopped
1 bunch fresh parsley, finely chopped
2 (4-ounce) jars chopped pimentos
8 to 10 sweet gherkins, finely chopped
1/4 cup sweet pickle juice

3/4 cup vegetable oil
1/2 to 3/4 cup spicy mustard
1 (32-ounce) jar mayonnaise
Salt and pepper to taste
Paprika to taste

Boil the unpeeled potatoes in water to cover in a large saucepan until tender. Drain and cool. Chill for 8 to 10 hours. Peel the potatoes and cut into 1/2-inch cubes. Combine the potatoes, celery, parsley, pimentos, pickles, pickle juice and oil in a large bowl and toss gently to combine. Add the mustard, mayonnaise, salt and pepper and mix well. Spoon into a large serving bowl. Sprinkle with paprika. Chill, covered, for 8 to 10 hours before serving.

Serves 12 to 15

Italian Bruschetta Salad

1 tablespoon garlic salt
1 tablespoon onion powder
1 tablespoon sugar
2 tablespoons dried oregano
1 teaspoon white pepper
1/4 teaspoon dried thyme
1 teaspoon dried basil
1 tablespoon dried parsley
1/4 cup white vinegar

2/3 cup canola oil
2 tablespoons water
1 (16-ounce) loaf dry Italian bread, torn
3 cups chopped seeded tomatoes
3/4 cup thinly sliced red onion
1/3 cup pitted black olives, cut into
  halves lengthwise
1/2 cup (2 ounces) shredded
  Parmesan cheese

Mix the garlic salt, onion powder, sugar, oregano, white pepper, thyme, basil and parsley in a small bowl. Whisk the vinegar, canola oil, water and 2 tablespoons of the seasoning mix in a bowl. Chill for 2 to 3 hours before serving. Store the remaining seasoning mix in an airtight container for another use. Combine the bread, tomatoes, onion and olives in a salad bowl. Add the cheese and toss to mix. Add the chilled salad dressing and toss to coat.

Serves 6 to 8

Winter Salad with Cambozola Crostini

1 loaf crusty bread	1 teaspoon white wine vinegar
1 wedge Cambozola or other soft ripe	1/2 cup extra-virgin olive oil
blue cheese	4 cups mixed greens
1 teaspoon Dijon mustard	1 cup dried cranberries
Pinch of sugar	1 cup chopped mushrooms
Juice of 1/2 lemon	1 cup chopped carrots
1 teaspoon minced garlic	Salt and pepper to taste

Cut the bread diagonally into eight slices and place on a baking sheet. Broil until the bread is toasted. Spread the cheese on the toasted bread. Whisk the Dijon mustard, sugar, lemon juice, garlic and vinegar in a bowl until blended. Whisk in the olive oil. Combine the mixed greens, dried cranberries, mushrooms and carrots in a large salad bowl. Add the dressing and toss to coat. Sprinkle with salt and pepper. Divide among four salad plates and top each with two slices of crostini.

Serves 4

Veggie Delight Pasta Salad

2 teaspoons salt	2 bunches asparagus, trimmed
2 teaspoons dried oregano	1 pound penne, cooked and drained
2 teaspoons dried parsley flakes	1 pint cherry tomatoes, cut into
2 teaspoons garlic powder	halves or quarters
1 1/2 teaspoons onion powder	1 1/2 cups (6 ounces) shaved
1 teaspoon freshly ground pepper	Parmesan cheese
4 large portobello mushroom caps	Lemon juice to taste
Olive oil	

Mix the salt, oregano, parsley flakes, garlic powder, onion powder and pepper in a bowl. Rub the mushroom caps lightly with olive oil. Grill over medium heat for 10 minutes or until tender, turning once. Toss the asparagus spears with olive oil. Grill for 5 to 10 minutes or until tender. Cut the grilled mushrooms and asparagus into bite-size pieces. Combine the mushrooms, asparagus, pasta, tomatoes, cheese, olive oil and lemon juice in a bowl and toss to coat. Add the seasoning mixture and toss to mix. Serve immediately.

Serves 8 to 12

Tropical Shrimp Pasta Salad

4 ounces fusilli pasta

3 tablespoons mayonnaise

3 tablespoons water

2 tablespoons horseradish

2 tablespoons Dijon mustard

1 garlic clove, chopped

12 ounces peeled cooked shrimp

4 cups torn leafy green lettuce

1/2 red bell pepper, sliced

1/2 yellow bell pepper, sliced

2 cups chopped ripe mangoes

1 tomato, finely chopped

2 large avocados, chopped

1/4 cup chopped fresh chives

Salt and pepper to taste

Cook the pasta in water to cover in a stockpot for 10 minutes or use the package directions; drain. Rinse the pasta with cold water and drain again. Mix the mayonnaise, 3 tablespoons water, the horseradish, Dijon mustard and garlic in a mixing bowl. Place one-half of the dressing in a salad bowl. Add the pasta and toss to coat. Add the shrimp to the remaining dressing and toss to mix.

Line two dinner plates with the lettuce. Spoon the pasta mixture over the lettuce. Place the bell pepper slices over the pasta. Spoon the shrimp mixture on top. Arrange the mangoes over the shrimp. Top with the tomato, avocados, chives, salt and pepper.

Serves 2

THE HARBOUR PLAYHOUSE

The Harbour Playhouse is a non-profit theatre located in Dickinson that offers a variety of live performances for Galveston County. It is a community theatre, which means the actors and actresses are volunteers. It also offers classes in performing arts for all age groups. This historic building was originally called "The Hollywood" when it first opened in 1941. It was renamed the Harbour Playhouse in 1991 and is a great asset to community arts.

The Galveston Restaurant Group owns some of Galveston Island's most popular restaurants. If you're hungry for delicious pizza and Italian cuisine, head over to Mario's or Papa's Pizza on the Seawall. If your taste buds are craving sushi, visit Sky Bar for the freshest selection in town. The Gumbo Bar blends Cajun seasonings with Gulf cuisine serving up gumbo and po' boys. Dine at Saltwater to enjoy seafood gourmet cuisine in a downtown setting.

Mario's Italian Tuna Salad

24 ounces steamed fresh tuna, or
2 (12-ounce) cans water-pack white albacore tuna, drained
1 (1-ounce) jar capers, drained
1/4 cup olive oil
1/4 teaspoon each salt and pepper
1/4 cup finely chopped red onion
3 ribs celery, chopped
2 Roma tomatoes, cut into wedges
Juice of 1 lemon

Mix the tuna, capers, olive oil, salt, pepper, onion, celery, tomatoes and lemon juice in a bowl. Chill for 30 minutes. Serve with crusty Italian bread.

Serves 6

Crab Meat Salad with Avocado

1 cup mayonnaise
1 teaspoon minced fresh parsley
1 teaspoon horseradish
1 tablespoon lemon juice
2 tablespoons ketchup
1 tablespoon Dijon mustard
1 pound fresh crab meat, shells removed and meat flaked
1 cup chopped peeled cucumber
1/2 cup chopped celery
1 avocado, sliced

Mix the mayonnaise, parsley, horseradish, lemon juice, ketchup and Dijon mustard in a bowl. Combine the crab meat, cucumber and celery in a bowl and mix well. Add the mayonnaise mixture and toss to coat. Spoon onto lettuce-lined plates. Top with the avocado.

Serves 4 to 6

Asian Chicken Salad

1 pound boneless skinless chicken breasts

1 teaspoon salt

1 tablespoon sesame oil

1/2 jalapeño chile, seeded and sliced

1 (1-inch) piece fresh ginger

2 cups water

3/4 cup chopped fresh mint

3/4 cup chopped fresh basil

3/4 cup chopped fresh cilantro

2 1/2 pounds shredded green cabbage

2 tablespoons cider vinegar

2 tablespoons fish sauce

1 1/2 tablespoons lime juice

2 teaspoons salt

3 large carrots, grated

3 radishes, grated

4 scallions, chopped

1 Granny Smith apple, grated

1 tablespoon sesame oil

Rub the chicken with 1 teaspoon salt and 1 tablespoon sesame oil. Bring the jalapeño chile, ginger and water to a simmer in a medium saucepan. Add the chicken. Simmer, covered, for 5 minutes. Turn off the heat. Steam for 5 minutes. Remove the chicken from the saucepan. Shred the chicken when cool enough to handle.

Mix the mint, basil and cilantro in a bowl. Combine the cabbage, vinegar, fish sauce, lime juice and 2 teaspoons salt in a large glass or stainless steel bowl and mix well. Let stand for 10 minutes. Add the carrots, radishes, scallions, apple and 1 1/2 cups of the herb mixture and mix well. Stir in 1 tablespoon sesame oil. Spoon onto serving plates. Top with the chicken and sprinkle with the remaining 1/2 cup herb mixture.

Serves 4

Chicken and Couscous Salad

2 tablespoons pine nuts

1¼ cups fat-free less-sodium
chicken broth

1 (6-ounce) package couscous, or

1 cup couscous

3 cups chopped cooked chicken
(about 12 ounces)

½ cup thinly sliced green onions

½ cup chopped radishes (about 3 large)

½ cup chopped seeded
peeled cucumber

¼ cup chopped fresh flat-leaf parsley

¼ cup white wine vinegar

1½ teaspoons extra-virgin olive oil

1 teaspoon ground cumin

2 teaspoons salt

⅛ teaspoon freshly ground pepper

1 garlic clove, minced

Toast the pine nuts in a dry skillet over medium-high heat until fragrant, stirring constantly. Bring the broth to a boil in a medium saucepan. Add the couscous gradually. Remove from the heat. Let stand for 5 minutes; fluff with a fork. Spoon into a large bowl and cool slightly. Add the chicken, green onions, radishes, cucumber, parsley and toasted pine nuts and toss gently. Whisk the vinegar, olive oil, cumin, salt, pepper and garlic in a bowl. Drizzle over the couscous salad and toss to coat.

Serves 4

Texas Beer Bread

2 cups self-rising flour

2 tablespoons sugar

1 bottle Ziegenbock beer or other
dark beer

Combine the flour, sugar and beer in a bowl and mix well. Spoon into a greased 5×9-inch loaf pan. Bake in a preheated 350-degree oven for 50 minutes. Serve warm with honey butter.

Makes 1 loaf

Rosemary Focaccia

1 envelope dry yeast
1 cup warm water
1 teaspoon sea salt
3 tablespoons olive oil
Pinch of sugar
2 1/2 cups all-purpose flour
3 tablespoons fresh rosemary, chopped
Olive oil for brushing
Coarse sea salt for sprinkling

Dissolve the yeast in the warm water in a bowl. Add 1 teaspoon sea salt, 3 tablespoons olive oil and the sugar and mix well. Stir in the flour in two or three increments to form a soft dough. Add the rosemary and mix well. Knead for several minutes on a lightly floured surface until smooth and elastic. Place in an oiled bowl, turning to coat the surface. Let rise, covered, in a warm place for 30 minutes or until doubled in bulk.

Roll on a lightly floured surface into one large or two small ovals about 1 1/2 inches thick. Make several cuts diagonally in the dough. Place on a well-oiled baking sheet. Brush with olive oil and sprinkle with coarse sea salt. Let rise for 15 minutes. Bake in a preheated 450-degree oven for 20 minutes or until light brown.

For Focaccia with Onions, Tomatoes and Mozzarella Cheese, omit the rosemary and top the dough with 1 small onion, sliced, 1 tablespoon chopped fresh oregano and mozzarella cheese to taste just before baking.

Serves 6 to 8

Chocolate Chip Orange Zucchini Bread

3 cups all-purpose flour
1/4 teaspoon baking powder
1 teaspoon baking soda
1 teaspoon salt
1/2 teaspoon cinnamon
1 teaspoon nutmeg
3 eggs
2 cups sugar

1 cup vegetable oil
2 teaspoons vanilla extract
2 cups grated zucchini
1 cup chopped walnuts
1 cup (6 ounces) semisweet
  chocolate chips
1 tablespoon grated orange zest

Sift the flour, baking powder, baking soda, salt, cinnamon and nutmeg together. Beat the eggs in a large mixing bowl until light and fluffy. Add the sugar and beat well. Stir in the oil, vanilla, zucchini, walnuts, chocolate chips and orange zest. Add the flour mixture and mix well. Spoon into two greased 5×9-inch loaf pans. Bake in a preheated 350-degree oven for 50 minutes or until the loaves test done. Invert onto wire racks to cool completely before slicing. These loaves freeze well.

Makes 2 loaves

Jalapeño Muffins

Margarine
2 cups all-purpose flour
2 tablespoons sugar
1 tablespoon baking powder
1/2 teaspoon salt
2 cups (8 ounces) shredded
  Cheddar cheese

2 tablespoons finely chopped
  jalapeño chiles
1 cup milk
1/4 cup vegetable oil
1 egg, lightly beaten

Grease the bottoms of twelve muffin cups with margarine. Mix the flour, sugar, baking powder, salt, Cheddar cheese and jalapeño chiles in a medium bowl. Add the milk, oil and egg and mix well. Fill the prepared muffin cups two-thirds full. Bake in a preheated 400-degree oven for 18 to 20 minutes or until golden brown.

Makes 1 dozen

Ham, Broccoli and Cheddar Muffins

1 1/2 cups baking mix
1 cup finely chopped cooked ham
1 1/2 cups (6 ounces) shredded
Cheddar cheese
1/2 cup (2 ounces) shredded Swiss cheese
1 (10-ounce) package frozen chopped broccoli,
thawed and well drained
1/2 cup milk
1 tablespoon butter, melted
1 egg, lightly beaten

Combine the baking mix, ham, 1 1/4 cups of the Cheddar cheese, the Swiss cheese and broccoli in a large bowl and mix well. Make a well in the center. Mix the milk, butter and egg in a bowl. Pour into the well in the baking mix mixture and stir just until moistened. Fill foil-lined muffin cups three-fourths full. Sprinkle with the remaining 1/4 cup Cheddar cheese. Bake in a preheated 425-degree oven for 18 minutes or until golden brown. Let stand for 2 to 3 minutes before removing from the pan.

Makes 1 dozen

Lighten Up

A Menu for a Healthy Meal

Appetizer
Shrimp Salsa 50

Salad
Cornucopia Salad 61

Entrée
Salmon with Fresh Tomato-Basil Relish 136

Side Dish
Green Bean Toss 147

Dessert
Blackberry Crisp 169

Birds of a Feather

POULTRY

In Southeast Texas, some of our dearest friends include the fine-feathered variety. To watch a big-billed pelican swoop down to get supper, or catch a glimpse of a reddish egret poking around in shallow water is a thrill only those privy to the coast get to enjoy.

Galveston's wetlands boast a slew of birds, fish, and plants, and we go to great lengths to preserve and protect them, as they rely on us for prosperity. In the mood for some bird watching? Whether you head over to Big Reef Nature Park, Kempner Park, or Galveston Island State Park, the show will not disappoint. If you would rather participate than just watch, Artist Boat may be up your alley. Take a kayak tour, explore Galveston Bay, and paint the images you see in a watercolor painting.

Grab a picnic basket, a pair of binoculars, and these recipes, and your Birds of a Feather will be a happy bunch.

Valeria Clarke

sponsor

Spiced Cider Chicken

12 cups (3 quarts) water

2 cups apple cider

1 bay leaf

1/4 cup kosher salt

1 tablespoon black peppercorns

1 (6-pound) chicken

2 cups apple cider

1 large onion, cut into halves

4 sprigs of flat-leaf parsley

4 garlic cloves

Bring the water, 2 cups apple cider, the bay leaf, salt and peppercorns to a boil in a saucepan. Boil until the salt dissolves, stirring constantly. Remove from the heat and cool completely. Discard the giblets and neck from the chicken cavity. Place the chicken in a 2-gallon sealable plastic bag. Add the brine and seal the bag. Marinate for 8 to 10 hours, turning the bag occasionally.

Bring 2 cups apple cider to a boil in a small saucepan over medium-high heat. Cook for 15 minutes or until thickened and reduced to 1/4 cup. Remove from the heat and set aside. Drain the chicken, discarding the brine. Pat the chicken dry with paper towels. Place the onion, parsley and garlic in the chicken cavity. Lift the wing tips up over the back and tuck under the chicken. Tie the legs. Place on a rack in a broiler pan. Bake in a preheated 400-degree oven for 1 1/2 hours or to 175 degrees on a meat thermometer. Remove from the oven. Remove the skin and discard. Baste the chicken with one-half of the reduced cider. Return to the oven and bake for 10 minutes. Remove from the oven and baste with the remaining cider. Place the chicken on a serving platter.

Place a sealable plastic bag inside a 2-cup glass measure. Pour the pan juices into the bag. Let stand for 10 minutes so the fat will rise to the top. Seal the bag and carefully snip off a bottom corner of the bag. Drain the drippings into a small bowl, stopping before the fat layer reaches the opening. Serve over the chicken.

Serves 8

Easy Breezy Chicken Cordon Bleu

6 boneless skinless chicken breasts	3 tablespoons olive oil
6 slices Swiss cheese	1/2 cup dry white wine
6 slices no-water-added ham	1 teaspoon chicken bouillon granules
1 cup all-purpose flour or bread crumbs	1 tablespoon cornstarch
1 teaspoon paprika	2 cups heavy cream or half-and-half
3 tablespoons butter	Chopped rosemary or basil to taste

Pound each chicken breast 1/4 to 1/2 inch thick. Place a cheese slice and ham slice on each to within 1/2 inch of the edges. Fold the edges over the filling and secure with wooden picks. Coat in a mixture of the flour and paprika. Melt the butter with the olive oil in a large skillet over medium-high heat. Add the chicken. Cook a few minutes on each side until brown. Place in a greased 9×13-inch baking pan, reserving the drippings in the skillet. Bake the chicken in a preheated 350-degree oven for 30 minutes. Stir the wine and bouillon granules into the reserved drippings in the skillet. Reduce the heat to low. Cook for 10 minutes, stirring constantly to scrape up the brown bits. Stir the cornstarch into the cream in a small bowl. Whisk gradually into the wine mixture. Cook over low heat until thickened, stirring constantly. Add rosemary. Pour over the chicken and serve warm.

Serves 6

Chicken Gillespie

1/2 cup all-purpose flour	1/3 cup grated Parmesan cheese
1/2 teaspoon salt	1/4 cup (1/2 stick) butter
1/2 teaspoon freshly ground pepper	1/2 cup white wine
4 boneless skinless chicken breasts	4 slices mozzarella cheese
2 eggs, beaten	Parsley to taste

Mix the flour, salt and pepper in a shallow dish. Dip each chicken breast into the flour mixture, then into the egg and finally into the Parmesan cheese to coat. Repeat the process if a thicker coating is desired. Melt the butter in a large saucepan over medium heat. Add the chicken breasts and sauté until golden brown. Add the wine. Cook for 10 minutes or until the chicken breasts are cooked through. Place a mozzarella cheese slice over each chicken breast. Cook, covered, for 3 minutes or until the mozzarella cheese melts. Sprinkle with parsley and serve.

Serves 4

Chicken Piccata

Galveston is one of the top locations for bird watching in the country. Galveston's terrain offers a favorable environment for both land and water birds. There are a variety of year-round birds, while rare species are seen migrating in the spring and fall. There are many places to bird watch on the island including Big Reef Nature Park, Kempner Park, Lafitte's Cove Nature Preserve, and the Galveston Island State Park.

2 boneless skinless whole chicken breasts
Salt and pepper to taste
All-purpose flour for dredging
3 tablespoons butter
1 tablespoon olive oil
2 garlic cloves, minced
8 ounces mushrooms, stemmed and thinly sliced
1/2 cup dry white wine
2 teaspoons fresh lemon juice
2 teaspoons drained water-pack capers

Pound the chicken breasts 1/4 inch thick. Sprinkle with salt and pepper. Dredge in flour to coat, shaking off any excess. Melt the butter with the olive oil in a sauté pan. Add the garlic and sauté briefly. Add the chicken and sauté for 2 minutes on each side or until light brown. Remove the chicken and set aside. Add the mushrooms to the pan drippings and sauté over medium heat for 1 minute. Return the chicken to the pan.

Stir in the wine and lemon juice. Simmer, covered, for 10 to 15 minutes or until the chicken is tender and cooked through. Add the capers. Cook until heated through. Place the chicken on a serving platter. Spoon the pan juices over the chicken. Garnish with chopped parsley and lemon slices. Serve with wild rice and a fresh vegetable.

Serves 2 to 4

Chipotle Chicken

1/4 cup extra-virgin olive oil

8 large garlic cloves, thinly sliced

2 yellow onions, chopped

1 cup ketchup

2 tablespoons Dijon mustard

2 tablespoons dark brown sugar

1/4 cup chopped canned chipotle chiles in adobo sauce

1 tablespoon Worcestershire sauce

2 tablespoons cider vinegar

1/2 teaspoon cinnamon

1 teaspoon salt

1/2 teaspoon pepper

2 chickens, cut into 8 pieces

Heat the olive oil in a 12-inch heavy skillet over medium-high heat until it shimmers. Add the garlic and sauté until golden brown. Remove the garlic with a slotted spoon to a plate. Reduce the heat to medium. Add the onions and cook for 15 minutes or until golden brown, stirring occasionally. Add the sautéed garlic, ketchup, Dijon mustard, brown sugar, chipotle chiles, Worcestershire sauce, vinegar, cinnamon, salt and pepper. Simmer for 25 minutes or until thickened, stirring occasionally.

Coat the chicken with one-half of the sauce. Place skin side up in an 11×17-inch baking pan. Bake on the middle oven rack in a preheated 450-degree oven for 25 minutes. Remove from the oven and brush with the remaining sauce. Bake for 20 to 25 minutes or until cooked through and well browned in spots.

Serves 6 to 8

Jamaican Grilled Jerk Chicken

3 scallions, chopped	1 tablespoon brown sugar
4 garlic cloves, chopped	1 tablespoon fresh thyme leaves
1 small white onion, chopped	2 teaspoons ground allspice
4 small habañero chiles, seeded	2 teaspoons pepper
1/4 cup fresh lime juice	3/4 teaspoons grated nutmeg
2 tablespoons soy sauce	1/2 teaspoon cinnamon
3 tablespoons olive oil	4 chicken breasts, cut into halves
1 1/2 tablespoons salt	3 pounds chicken thighs and drumsticks

Process the scallions, garlic, onion, habañero chiles, lime juice, soy sauce, olive oil, salt, brown sugar, thyme, allspice, pepper, nutmeg and cinnamon in a blender until smooth. Divide the chicken and marinade between two sealable plastic bags. Seal the bags, pressing out the excess air and turning the bags several times to evenly distribute the marinade. Place the bags in a shallow pan. Marinate in the refrigerator for 24 hours, turning once or twice. Bring the chicken to room temperature. Drain the chicken, discarding the marinade. Preheat the grill to high and then reduce the heat to medium. Grill the chicken for 15 to 20 minutes or until brown on all sides. Reduce the heat to low. Grill, covered, for 25 minutes longer or until the chicken is cooked through.

To roast in the oven, place the chicken in two large shallow baking pans. Bake on the upper and lower thirds of a preheated 400-degree oven for 40 to 45 minutes or until cooked through, switching the positions of the pans halfway through.

Serves 8

Mediterranean Chicken

1 cup stewed tomatoes   1/4 cup black olives
1 cup tomato sauce   1/2 cup chopped onion
1 tablespoon capers   1/2 cup mushrooms, sliced
1 tablespoon garlic   8 ounces chicken breasts

Combine the tomatoes, tomato sauce, capers, garlic, olives, onion and mushrooms in a bowl and mix well. Place the chicken in a glass 9×13-inch baking dish. Pour the tomato mixture over the chicken. Bake in a preheated 350-degree oven for 45 to 60 minutes or until the chicken is cooked through.

Serves 4

Southern Garlic Fried Chicken

4 boneless skinless chicken breasts   1/2 cup seasoned bread crumbs
2 teaspoons garlic powder   1 cup all-purpose flour
1 teaspoon black pepper   1/2 cup milk
1 teaspoon cayenne pepper   1 egg
1 teaspoon salt   1 cup vegetable oil
1 teaspoon paprika

Pound the chicken until thin. Mix the garlic powder, black pepper, cayenne pepper, salt, paprika, bread crumbs and flour in a shallow dish. Whisk the milk and egg in a shallow dish. Heat the oil in an electric skillet at 350 degrees or in a heavy frying pan. Dip the chicken into the egg mixture and then dredge in the flour mixture to coat evenly. Add to the hot oil. Fry for 5 minutes on each side or until the chicken is cooked through and the juices run clear.

Serves 4

Maple Barbecued Chicken

Maple Barbecue Sauce
2 large onions, finely chopped
2$^1/_2$ tablespoons vegetable oil
2$^1/_2$ tablespoons Worcestershire sauce
1 tablespoon Dijon mustard
1$^1/_4$ cups ketchup
2$^1/_2$ cups chicken broth
$^3/_4$ cup cider vinegar
$^1/_2$ cup pure maple syrup

Chicken
$^1/_2$ cup white wine vinegar
1 tablespoon salt
1 cup vegetable oil
5 whole chicken breasts, cut into halves
10 chicken thighs
10 chicken drumsticks
10 chicken wings

To prepare the barbecue sauce, combine the onions, oil, Worcestershire sauce, Dijon mustard, ketchup, broth, vinegar and maple syrup in a large heavy saucepan and mix well. Bring to a boil. Reduce the heat and simmer for 50 minutes, stirring occasionally.

To prepare the chicken, whisk the vinegar and salt in a bowl. Whisk in the oil in a fine stream until emulsified. Divide the chicken between two large bowls. Pour the marinade over the chicken. Chill, covered, for 8 to 10 hours. Drain the chicken, discarding the marinade. Place the chicken on a grill rack. Grill 4 inches above the hot coals for 10 minutes on each side or until cooked through. Baste with some of the barbecue sauce. Grill for 2 minutes longer. Serve with the remaining barbecue sauce.

Serves 20

Stuffed Chicken Breasts

1 (12-ounce) jar marinated artichoke hearts,
drained and coarsely chopped
1 cup shredded fontina cheese
1/2 cup packed drained coarsely chopped oil-pack
sun-dried tomatoes
1 tablespoon dried basil
4 (5-ounce) boneless skinless chicken breasts
1/8 teaspoon salt
1/8 teaspoon pepper
2 tablespoons olive oil

Mix the artichoke hearts, cheese, sun-dried tomatoes and basil in a medium bowl.

Cut a slit horizontally into the side of each chicken breast using a small sharp knife to form a pocket. Stuff the cheese mixture into each pocket. Sprinkle with salt and pepper. Heat the olive oil in an ovenproof heavy skillet over medium-high heat. Add the chicken breasts. Cook for 4 minutes on each side or until brown. Bake in a preheated 375-degree oven for 15 to 17 minutes or until cooked through.

Serves 4

Galveston County is surrounded by bountiful wetlands that house many species of birds, fish, and plants. Wetland habitats are among the most biologically productive systems on the planet. Galveston Bay's commercial and recreational fish species rely on the wetlands for prosperity. The wetlands not only provide beautiful scenery but also compose 60 percent of Galveston Bay's 232 miles of shoreline to prevent and reduce erosion. It is breathtaking to watch the sun setting over the wetlands.

Zesty Chicken

6 limes

6 boneless skinless chicken breasts

$^1/_2$ cup fresh lemon juice

7 tablespoons all-purpose flour

2 teaspoons paprika

1 teaspoon salt

1 teaspoon pepper

1 tablespoon olive oil

$^1/_3$ cup packed brown sugar

$^1/_4$ cup chicken broth

12 thin orange slices

Grate 2 tablespoons zest from the limes and set aside. Squeeze enough juice from the limes to measure $^3/_4$ cup. Place the chicken in a large sealable plastic bag. Pour the lime juice and lemon juice over the chicken and seal the bag. Marinate in the refrigerator for 2 hours.

Drain the chicken, reserving 2 tablespoons of the marinade. Pat the chicken dry with paper towels. Mix the flour, paprika, salt and pepper in a shallow dish. Dredge the chicken in the flour mixture. Heat 1$^1/_2$ teaspoons of the olive oil in a large nonstick skillet coated with nonstick cooking spray over medium-high heat. Add one-half of the chicken. Cook for 2 minutes on each side or until light brown. Place in a 9×13-inch baking dish coated with nonstick cooking spray. Repeat with the remaining 1$^1/_2$ teaspoons olive oil and the remaining chicken.

Mix the lime zest with the brown sugar and sprinkle over the chicken. Blend the reserved marinade with the broth and drizzle around the chicken. Top each chicken breast with two orange slices. Bake in a preheated 350-degree oven for 25 minutes or until the chicken is cooked through. Strain any of the remaining liquid and spoon over the chicken to serve.

Serves 6

Artist Boat is a nonprofit organization that promotes awareness and preservation of the coastal and marine environments. It was founded in 2003 and provides guided tours of Galveston Bay by kayak to showcase Galveston's natural beauties. The tours include lessons on kayaking, environmental education activities, exploration of Galveston Bay and its marine/coastal life, and concludes with an opportunity to create a watercolor painting. Artist Boat is fun and beneficial for people of all ages.

Lemon Caper Chicken

2 1/2 pounds boneless skinless chicken tenders
1 tablespoon chopped garlic
1/4 teaspoon salt
1/4 teaspoon pepper
1/2 cup Italian bread crumbs
1/4 cup (1 ounce) shredded Parmesan cheese
1/3 cup olive oil
2 cups chicken broth
1/2 cup pinot grigio
1/4 cup capers, drained and rinsed
1 large lemon, thinly sliced and seeds removed
1/4 cup (1 ounce) shredded Parmesan cheese

Mix the chicken, garlic, salt and pepper in a bowl. Mix the bread crumbs and 1/4 cup Parmesan cheese in a shallow dish. Dredge the chicken in the bread crumb mixture to coat well. Cook in the olive oil in a skillet for 3 minutes on each side or until brown. Place in a 10×13-inch baking pan.

Pour the broth and wine over the chicken. Sprinkle with the capers. Place the lemon slices over the chicken. Sprinkle with 1/4 cup Parmesan cheese. Bake, covered, in a preheated 375-degree oven for 30 minutes. Uncover and bake for 30 minutes longer or until the chicken is cooked through.

Serves 6

Baked Chicken Flautas with Cilantro Cream Sauce

Cilantro Cream Sauce

1 cup sour cream

Juice of 1 or 2 limes

1 jalapeño chile, seeded and minced

1/2 cup cilantro leaves

Salt and pepper to taste

Flautas

1 small onion, chopped

1/2 teaspoon butter

1 pound boneless skinless chicken breasts, cooked and shredded

2 cups (8 ounces) shredded Monterey Jack cheese

1 teaspoon garlic powder

1 teaspoon cumin

10 flour tortillas

To prepare the sauce, process the sour cream, lime juice, jalapeño chile and cilantro in a food processor or blender until blended. Season with salt and pepper.

To prepare the flautas, sauté the onion in the butter in a skillet over medium to high heat until translucent. Combine the sautéed onion, chicken, cheese, garlic powder and cumin in a bowl and mix well. Spray a baking sheet with nonstick cooking spray. Spoon the chicken mixture down the center of each tortilla and roll up tightly. Place seam side down on the prepared baking sheet. Spray the tops with nonstick cooking spray. Bake in a preheated 375-degree oven for 8 minutes on each side or until golden brown. Garnish with cilantro. Serve with the sauce.

Serves 8

King Ranch Chicken

1 (5-pound) chicken
2 ribs celery, cut into 3 pieces each
2 carrots, cut into 3 pieces each
1 tablespoon salt
2 tablespoons butter
1 onion, chopped
1 green bell pepper, chopped
1 garlic clove, pressed
1 (10-ounce) can cream of
  mushroom soup

1 (10-ounce) can cream of chicken soup
2 (10-ounce) cans tomatoes with
  green chiles, drained
1 teaspoon dried oregano
1 teaspoon Mexican chile powder
1 teaspoon ground cumin
3 cups (12 ounces) shredded sharp
  Cheddar cheese
12 fajita-size corn tortillas, cut into
  1/2-inch strips

Remove the giblets from the chicken. Place the chicken, celery, carrots and salt in a large Dutch oven and cover with water. Bring to a boil over medium-high heat. Reduce the heat to low. Simmer, covered, for 50 to 60 minutes or until the chicken is cooked through. Remove from the heat. Remove the chicken from the broth to cool. Reserve 3/4 cup of the broth.

Melt the butter in a large skillet over medium-high heat. Add the onion. Sauté for 6 to 7 minutes or until tender. Add the bell pepper and garlic. Sauté for 3 to 4 minutes or until tender. Stir in the reserved broth, mushroom soup, chicken soup, tomatoes with green chiles, oregano, chile powder and cumin. Cook for 8 minutes, stirring occasionally.

Shred the chicken into bite-size pieces, discarding the skin and bones. Layer one-half of the chicken in a lightly greased 9×13-inch baking dish. Cover with one-half of the soup mixture and sprinkle with 1 cup of the cheese. Cover with one-half of the tortilla strips. Repeat the layers once. Sprinkle with the remaining 1 cup cheese. Bake in a preheated 350-degree oven for 55 to 60 minutes or until bubbly. Let stand for 10 minutes before serving. For a quicker version, use a 2-pound deli-roasted chicken and 3/4 cup chicken broth, omitting the celery, carrots and salt.

Serves 8 to 10

Creamed Chicken Casserole

1 package chicken-flavored rice and vermicelli mix
with chicken broth and herbs
1 tablespoon butter or margarine
2$\frac{1}{4}$ cups hot water
1$\frac{1}{2}$ pounds boneless skinless chicken breasts,
cut into bite-size pieces
1 cup fresh mushrooms
$\frac{1}{2}$ teaspoon garlic powder
$\frac{3}{4}$ cup sour cream
$\frac{1}{4}$ teaspoon salt
$\frac{1}{4}$ teaspoon pepper
1 (10-ounce) can cream of mushroom soup
$\frac{1}{4}$ cup crushed multigrain crackers
1 tablespoon margarine, melted

Cook the rice mix in a large nonstick skilled using the package directions, using the butter and hot water. Remove from the skillet and set aside. Wipe the skillet with a paper towel. Coat the skillet with nonstick cooking spray and heat over high heat. Add the chicken, mushrooms and garlic powder. Sauté for 6 minutes or until the chicken is cooked through.

Combine the rice mixture, chicken mixture, sour cream, salt, pepper and soup in a bowl and mix well. Spoon into a 2-quart baking dish coated with nonstick cooking spray. Mix the cracker crumbs with the margarine. Sprinkle over the chicken mixture. Bake in a preheated 350-degree oven for 35 minutes or until heated through.

Serves 6

Mexican Chicken and Rice

6 chicken breasts	2 tomatoes, chopped
1 teaspoon salt	3¹/₂ cups chicken broth
1 teaspoon pepper	1 cup beer
1 teaspoon garlic salt	1 teaspoon salt
1 small onion, finely chopped	¹/₂ teaspoon pepper
1 red bell pepper, chopped	2 teaspoons saffron
1 small green bell pepper, chopped	1 teaspoon cumin
2 tablespoons minced garlic	2 cups uncooked rice
¹/₄ cup olive oil	1 cup frozen peas
1 cup chopped ham	1 pound asparagus, trimmed

Place the chicken, 1 teaspoon salt, 1 teaspoon pepper and the garlic salt in a saucepan and cover with water. Bring to a boil and cook until the chicken is cooked through. Drain the chicken and set aside to cool. Shred the chicken into small pieces, discarding the skin and bones.

Sauté the onion, bell peppers and garlic in the olive oil in a skillet until the onion is translucent. Add the chicken, ham and tomatoes. Add the broth, beer, 1 teaspoon salt, ¹/₂ teaspoon pepper, the saffron and cumin. Bring to a boil. Add the rice and return to a boil. Cook, covered, over low heat for 30 minutes. Add the peas and asparagus. Cook, covered, for 5 minutes. Spoon onto a platter and serve. The recipe can be made in advance, spooned into a baking dish and reheated in a preheated 350-degree oven until warmed through.

Serves 8

Cheesy Chicken Chili

1 pound ground chicken or turkey
1 sweet onion, chopped
3 garlic cloves, finely chopped
3 tablespoons olive oil
1 (10-ounce) can tomatoes with green chiles
1 (32-ounce) can white cannellini beans, drained and rinsed
1 (14-ounce) can white and yellow whole kernel corn
2 cups chicken broth
1 1/2 tablespoons ground cumin
1 tablespoon chili powder
1 teaspoon chipotle chile powder
1 teaspoon salt
1 teaspoon coarsely ground pepper
1 cup sour cream
12 ounces Velveeta cheese, cubed
3 tablespoons cilantro
1 (10-ounce) can cream of chile poblano soup

Sauté the chicken with the onion and garlic in the olive oil in a stockpot until the chicken is cooked through. Add the tomatoes with green chiles, beans, corn, broth, cumin, chili powder, chipotle chile powder, salt and pepper and mix well. Simmer for 20 minutes. Stir in the sour cream, Velveeta, cilantro and poblano soup. Simmer until heated through and bubbly. Serve with corn bread, corn chips or tortillas.

Serves 8

GALVESTON ISLAND STATE PARK

The Galveston Island State Park is located on the west end of Galveston Island. It includes more than 2,000 acres of land and was opened in 1975 as a state park. The park offers camping, bird watching, hiking, mountain bike riding, fishing, and beach swimming. It also offers educational tours of the beach and bay areas by appointment. This state park houses wading and shore birds, mallards, raccoons, armadillos, and rabbits.

Lafitte's Pasta

2 tablespoons butter or margarine
2 cups cooked turkey or chicken
3/4 cup undrained canned mushrooms
1/4 cup chopped fresh parsley
1 1/2 garlic cloves, minced
1/4 cup dry white wine
6 tablespoons butter or margarine
1/2 cup (2 ounces) grated Parmesan cheese
2/3 cup milk
Pepper to taste
8 ounces capellini, cooked and drained

Melt 2 tablespoons butter in a large skillet. Add the turkey, mushrooms, parsley and garlic. Cook until the turkey is brown. Add the wine. Cook for 3 minutes, stirring constantly. Spoon into a small bowl. Melt 6 tablespoons butter in the skillet. Add the cheese, milk and pepper. Cook over low heat until the cheese melts and the sauce is smooth, stirring constantly. Remove from the heat. Combine the cheese sauce and turkey mixture with the pasta and toss gently.

Serves 4 to 6

Almond Turkey Tenderloin

1/3 cup slivered almonds, toasted

3 tablespoons panko (Japanese bread crumbs)

1 1/2 pounds turkey tenderloins

Salt and pepper to taste

2 tablespoons olive oil

1/4 cup dry sherry

4 teaspoons all-purpose flour

1 cup chicken broth

1 tablespoon unsalted butter

1/4 cup slivered almonds, toasted

2 tablespoons chopped fresh parsley

Process 1/3 cup almonds in a food processor until finely ground. Mix with the panko in a shallow dish. Sprinkle the turkey with salt and pepper. Roll in the panko mixture to coat well. Heat the olive oil in a sauté pan over medium to high heat for 2 minutes or until hot enough to sear. Add the turkey and sear for 5 minutes or until golden brown. Turn and sauté for 5 to 8 minutes longer or until cooked through. Remove the turkey to a baking sheet and keep warm in a preheated 250-degree oven.

Whisk the sherry and flour in a bowl until thick. Heat the broth with the pan drippings in the sauté pan, stirring to scrape up the brown bits from the bottom of the pan. Whisk in the sherry mixture. Boil for 1 minute. Reduce the heat and simmer until thickened, whisking constantly. Whisk in the butter until melted. Stir in the almonds and parsley. Spoon the sauce over the turkey on a serving platter.

Serves 4

THE REDDISH EGRET

The reddish egret is Galveston Island's official city bird. It ranges from medium to large in size and is often seen in shallow saltwater. The reddish egret comes in a dark and a white form; its bill is pink at the base and black at the tip. It is a very active forager, often seen running, jumping, and in pursuit of fish. This species only nests in Texas, Louisiana, and Florida.

Fiesta Texas

A Menu for a
Scrumptious Mexican Dinner

Appetizer
Crab Meat Guacamole 47

Soup
Black Bean Soup 59

Entrée
Baked Chicken Flautas with
Cilantro Cream Sauce 91

Side Dish
Cheesy Cream Corn with Cilantro 150

Dessert
Mexican Chocolate Cake 176

Divine Red and White

BEEF, PORK, WILD GAME

To ride down the road and see the Gulf of Mexico on your left and a ranch on your right would not be out of the ordinary in Galveston. Here we get to enjoy a melting pot mixed with ranching, farming, and our coastal-western heritage. In the 1800s ranching was an integral part of our economy. Our abundant wetlands and mineral-rich soil provided ideal conditions for crop growing and herding cattle. Take a ride to Galveston's West End and get a glimpse of the coastal old west.

Have something more exotic in mind? Head over to the Bayou Wildlife Park in Alvin where animals and birds from Africa, India, Asia, and Australia run free. If getting a taste of history is what you like, make your way to the Butler Museum in League City, where the Butler Longhorn bloodline is preserved and honored.

Here in Divine Red and White, we invite you to taste the beef, pork, and wild game that make up our delicious heritage.

Lawrence R. Clarke, M.D.
sponsor

Filets Mignons with Cabernet Sauce

The Bayou Wildlife Park is located in Alvin, Texas, and is eighty acres of natural habitat. It is privately owned and has been in existence for more than thirty years. There are fifty species of animals and birds from places like Africa, India, Asia, Australia, and North and South America. The park offers guided tram rides with opportunities to learn about the animals and feed them. Petting zoos, alligator ponds, and monkey islands are also included in the park.

1 tablespoon cold butter
4 (4-ounce) filets mignons
1/4 teaspoon salt, or to taste
1/4 teaspoon pepper, or to taste
1 tablespoon cold butter
1/3 cup chopped shallots
2/3 cup cabernet sauvignon
1 tablespoon drained capers
1 tablespoon Dijon mustard
1/3 cup chopped fresh parsley
2 tablespoons cold butter

Melt 1 tablespoon butter in a large heavy skillet over medium-high heat. Sprinkle both sides of the steaks with 1/4 teaspoon salt and 1/4 teaspoon pepper. Add to the melted butter. Cook for 4 minutes on each side for medium or to the desired degree of doneness. Remove to individual serving plates and tent with foil to keep warm.

Melt 1 tablespoon butter in the pan drippings over medium-high heat. Add the shallots. Sauté for 1 minute. Add the wine, capers and Dijon mustard. Simmer for 2 minutes or until slightly thickened, stirring constantly. Stir in the parsley. Reduce the heat to medium-low. Whisk in the remaining 2 tablespoons butter. Sprinkle with salt and pepper to taste. Serve over the steaks.

Serves 4

Steak with Corn Salsa

Corn Salsa

3 cups fresh whole kernel corn

White portions of 4 scallions, sliced

2 garlic cloves, minced

1 teaspoon kosher salt

1/2 teaspoon cumin

1/2 teaspoon chili powder

1/4 teaspoon pepper

2 tablespoons unsalted butter

2 plum tomatoes, finely chopped

1 fresh jalapeño chile, finely chopped

1/4 cup finely chopped fresh cilantro

Green portions of 4 scallions, sliced

Steak

1/2 teaspoon kosher salt

1 teaspoon cumin

1/2 teaspoon chili powder

1/4 teaspoon pepper

2 pounds trimmed boneless sirloin steak,
  about 1 1/2 inches thick

To prepare the salsa, heat a large cast-iron skillet over medium-high heat until hot. Add the corn. Roast for 8 to 10 minutes or until golden brown, stirring occasionally. Spoon into a bowl. Sauté the white portions of the scallions with the garlic, salt, cumin, chili powder and pepper in the butter in the skillet over medium heat for 3 to 4 minutes or until tender. Remove from the heat. Stir in the corn, tomatoes and jalapeño chile. Just before serving, reheat over medium heat, stirring occasionally. Stir in the cilantro and the green portions of the scallions.

To prepare the steak, mix the salt, cumin, chili powder and pepper together. Sprinkle on both sides of the steak and place on a grill rack. Grill for 18 to 20 minutes for medium-rare or to 140 degrees on a meat thermometer. Remove to a grooved cutting board and let stand for 5 to 10 minutes before slicing. Spoon the salsa over the sliced steak and top with any accumulated juices.

Serves 4

Rolled Flank Steak

2 pounds beef flank steak
1/4 cup soy sauce
1/2 cup olive oil
2 teaspoons steak seasoning
8 ounces thinly sliced provolone cheese
4 slices thick-cut bacon
1/4 cup fresh spinach leaves
1/2 red bell pepper, cut into strips
1/2 cup sliced cremini

Place the steak on a cutting board with the short end closest to you. Cut through the steak horizontally to within 1/2 inch of the opposite side to butterfly. (You may ask the butcher to do this for you.) Mix the soy sauce, olive oil and steak seasoning in a gallon-size sealable plastic bag. Add the steak and seal the bag. Marinate in the refrigerator for 2 hours; drain, discarding the marinade.

Lay the steak flat in front of you with the grain running from left to right. Layer the cheese across the steak, leaving a 1-inch border. Arrange the bacon, spinach, bell pepper and mushrooms across the cheese in stripes running in the same direction as the grain. Roll the steak firmly up and away from you to enclose the fillings, being careful not to squeeze the fillings out the ends. Secure with wooden picks. Place in a greased glass baking dish. Bake in a preheated 350-degree oven for 1 hour or to 145 degrees on a meat thermometer. Remove from the oven and let stand for 5 to 10 minutes. Cut into 1-inch slices, discarding the wooden picks before serving.

Serves 6

South American Grilled Flank Steak

1/4 cup soy sauce	1/3 cup cilantro, chopped
1 tablespoon grated fresh ginger	1/3 cup mint leaves, chopped
1 tablespoon honey	1/4 cup chopped green onions
1 tablespoon sesame oil	3 tablespoons water
1 garlic clove, minced	1 tablespoon fresh lime juice
1/4 tablespoon ground pepper	2 teaspoons olive oil
1 pound flank steak	1 garlic clove, minced

Process the soy sauce, ginger, honey, sesame oil, one garlic clove and the pepper in a blender or food processor until smooth. Place the steak in a sealable plastic bag. Add the marinade and seal the bag. Shake to coat. Marinate in the refrigerator for 15 minutes or up to 24 hours. Drain the steak, discarding the marinade. Place the steak on a grill rack. Grill over medium-high heat for 5 minutes on each side for medium or to the desired degree of doneness. Remove from the heat. Let stand for 10 minutes.

Process the cilantro, mint, green onions, water, lime juice, olive oil and one garlic clove in a blender or food processor until smooth. Cut the steak crosswise into 1/4-inch slices and drizzle with the cilantro sauce.

Serves 4

Beef Brisket

1 large beef brisket	1/2 to 1 cup water
1 (4-ounce) jar Pickapeppa sauce	Salt and pepper to taste
1 (4-ounce) jar liquid smoke	10 garlic cloves (optional)

Trim any excess fat from the brisket. Place the brisket in a large baking pan. Add the Pickapeppa sauce, liquid smoke, water, salt, pepper and garlic. Cover with foil. Bake in a preheated 250-degree oven for 7 to 10 hours or to the desired degree of doneness, checking after 7 hours. Drain the brisket, reserving the pan juices in a separate dish. Chill the brisket and pan juices separately until cool. Cut the brisket into slices. Skim the fat from the pan juices. Pour the pan juices over the brisket. Bake in a preheated 200- to 250-degree oven until heated through.

Serves 8 to 10

The Butler Museum houses a vast collection of unique western art, science exhibits, and historic memorabilia documenting the seven bloodlines of longhorn cattle. It is located on ten acres in League City's historic district in Heritage Park. The Butler Museum's main purpose is to preserve the history of the Butler Longhorn bloodline and honor the early settlers of League City. Its name is derived from Milby Butler, who led the preservation of Texas longhorn cattle from extinction.

Spiced Beef Tenderloin

2 pounds trimmed and tied center-cut beef tenderloin roast
1 1/2 teaspoons black peppercorns
1 1/2 teaspoons coriander seeds
1 1/2 teaspoons cumin seeds
1 1/2 teaspoons brown mustard seeds
1/2 teaspoon whole cloves
1/2 teaspoon fennel seeds
1 (1 1/2-inch) stick of cinnamon, broken into small pieces
1 1/4 teaspoons coarse sea salt or kosher salt
1 1/2 tablespoons vegetable oil

Let the roast stand at room temperature for 30 minutes. Combine the peppercorns, coriander seeds, cumin seeds, mustard seeds, cloves, fennel seeds, cinnamon and salt in a 10-inch heavy skillet and mix well. Toast over medium-low heat for 3 to 5 minutes or until the mustard seeds begin to pop, stirring occasionally. Remove from the heat and cool completely. Grind the toasted mixture in a clean coffee grinder, blender or food processor.

Pat the roast dry. Rub the spice mixture all over the roast, including the ends. Heat the oil in a skillet over high heat until the oil shimmers. Add the roast. Cook for 10 minutes, turning frequently until brown on all sides. Place the roast in a small roasting pan. Bake on the middle oven rack in a preheated 350-degree oven for 25 to 35 minutes or to 135 degrees on a meat thermometer inserted 2 inches into the center of the roast for medium-rare. Remove to a cutting board. Let stand for 10 minutes. Remove the string and cut the roast into slices.

Serves 4 to 6

Grandma's Pot Roast

3 carrots, cut into 1/2-inch slices
3 ribs celery, cut into 1/2-inch slices
1 (3-pound) pot roast, shoulder roast, brisket, or
any large relatively lean cut of beef
Salt and pepper to taste
1 white onion, sliced and separated into rings
1 (14-ounce) can diced tomatoes, drained
2 potatoes
Paprika to taste

Place the carrots and celery in the center of a large roasting pan. Place the roast fat side up on top of the vegetables. Sprinkle with salt and pepper. Layer the onion rings over the beef. Pour the tomatoes over the onion rings. Bake, covered, in a preheated 275-degree oven for 3 hours. Peel the potatoes and cut into large chunks. Sprinkle each chunk with paprika. Remove the roast from the oven. Place the potato chunks around the roast in the pan juices. Cover and return to the oven. Bake for 45 minutes longer or until the roast is fork-tender.

Serves 4

The Farmers' Market is located in Historic Downtown of Galveston in Saengerfest Park. It began in 2007 and quickly became a very popular event among locals and tourists. The market is organized by the Historic Downtown Partnership and manned by volunteers. The event takes place on the second Saturday of the month from April through December. Vendors offer a wide variety of organic produce, handmade crafts, and flowers. Attending the market is a great way to support the local farmers.

Zinfandel-Braised Beef Short Ribs

4 pounds beef short ribs, bone in, cut into single rib chops
Sea salt and freshly ground pepper to taste
3 cups red zinfandel
1/2 cup sugar
1 tablespoon minced fresh garlic
3 sprigs of fresh thyme
Pinch of salt
6 tablespoons canola oil
2 cups chopped onions
1/2 cup each chopped celery and chopped carrots
3/4 cup canned chopped tomatoes
2 cups beef broth
2 ounces porcini mushrooms
2 bay leaves

Sprinkle the ribs generously with salt and pepper. Whisk the wine, sugar, garlic, thyme and pinch of salt in a large bowl. Add the ribs. Marinate, covered, in the refrigerator for 12 hours; drain, reserving the marinade. Let the ribs stand until room temperature. Brown the ribs in the oil in a Dutch oven over high heat for several minutes on each side, stirring carefully to turn frequently. Remove the ribs from the Dutch oven.

Add the onions, celery and carrots to the pan drippings. Cook for 10 minutes, stirring constantly. Reduce the heat to medium if the onions are browning too quickly. Return the ribs to the Dutch oven. Add the reserved marinade. Bring to a boil; reduce the heat. Simmer for several minutes, skimming the foam and fat from the surface. Add the tomatoes, broth, mushrooms and bay leaves. Simmer, uncovered, for 5 hours or until the ribs are fork-tender and nearly falling from the bones. Remove the ribs to a dish and cover to keep warm.

Simmer the pan liquids for 30 minutes or until reduced and able to coat the back of a spoon. Strain the braising liquid; return the ribs to the liquid. Season with salt and pepper. The beef may be prepared 3 to 4 days in advance. Reheat in the oven or microwave until the beef is 160 degrees.

Serves 6

Garlic Mustard Beef Skewers

2 pounds beef tenderloin	1/4 teaspoon kosher salt
4 garlic cloves, minced	1/4 teaspoon pepper
1/4 cup grainy mustard	1 tablespoon soy sauce
2 tablespoons Dijon mustard	2 tablespoons white wine vinegar
2 teaspoons paprika	1 tablespoon honey

Soak one package of 6-inch wooden skewers in cold water for 30 minutes; drain. Cut the tenderloin into halves. Cut each half into 1-inch slices. Skewer two beef slices onto two skewers so the beef lies flat. Repeat with the remaining beef. Whisk the garlic, grainy mustard, Dijon mustard, paprika, salt, pepper, soy sauce, vinegar and honey in a small bowl. Let stand, covered, for 30 minutes. Brush the beef liberally on both sides with the mustard mixture. Grill over high heat for 2 to 3 minutes on each side or until golden brown and medium-rare, brushing with the remaining mustard mixture.

Serves 4 to 6

Provençal Beef

12 garlic cloves	2 cups coarsely chopped carrots
2 teaspoons olive oil	1 1/2 cups chopped onions
2 pounds beef stew meat	1/2 cup beef broth
1/2 teaspoon salt	1 tablespoon tomato paste
1/4 teaspoon pepper	1 teaspoon chopped fresh rosemary
1 cup red wine	1 teaspoon chopped fresh thyme
1 teaspoon salt	1 (14-ounce) can petite-diced tomatoes
1/4 teaspoon pepper	1 bay leaf

Cook the garlic in the olive oil in a Dutch oven over low heat for 5 minutes, stirring occasionally. Remove the garlic. Increase the heat to medium-high. Add the beef, 1/2 teaspoon salt and 1/4 teaspoon pepper. Cook for 5 minutes or until the beef is brown. Remove the beef to a bowl and keep warm. Add the wine to the pan drippings and bring to a boil. Add the garlic, beef, 1 teaspoon salt, 1/4 teaspoon pepper, the carrots, onions, broth, tomato paste, rosemary, thyme, tomatoes and bay leaf and bring to a boil. Cover and bake in a preheated 300-degree oven for 2 1/2 hours. Discard the bay leaf. Serve with egg noodles or mashed potatoes.

Serves 6 to 8

Enchilada Casserole

1 pound ground round
1/2 cup chopped onion
4 teaspoons chili powder
1 1/2 teaspoons ground cumin
1/2 teaspoon freshly ground pepper
2 garlic cloves, minced
1 cup water
1 (11-ounce) jar mild taco sauce
6 corn tortillas
1 1/4 cups (5 ounces) shredded 2 percent sharp
Cheddar cheese

Brown the ground beef with the onion in a skillet over medium heat, stirring until crumbly; drain. Add the chili powder, cumin, pepper, garlic and water. Simmer for 10 minutes or until the water has evaporated and the mixture is thick.

Cover the bottom of a 9×13-inch baking dish with one-half of the taco sauce. Place three of the tortillas in the sauce, cutting the tortillas to fit the dish if needed. Spread the ground beef mixture over the tortillas. Sprinkle with 1/2 cup of the cheese. Drizzle the remaining taco sauce over the cheese. Top with the remaining three tortillas. Sprinkle with the remaining 3/4 cup cheese.

Bake, covered with foil, in a preheated 375-degree oven for 25 minutes. Remove the foil and bake for 5 minutes longer. Garnish with chopped green onions. Serve with shredded lettuce, chopped tomatoes and fat-free sour cream, if desired.

Serves 8 to 10

Jalapeño Steak

1 pound ground beef	1 onion, chopped
Salt and pepper to taste	1 (15-ounce) can tomatoes
1 jalapeño chile, finely chopped	1 cup (4 ounces) shredded mild
1 bell pepper, chopped	Cheddar cheese

Shape the ground beef into four patties 1/4 inch thick. Sprinkle with salt and pepper. Mix the jalapeño chile, bell pepper, onion, undrained tomatoes and cheese in a bowl. Brown two of the ground beef patties lightly in a skillet. Do not overcook. Place each patty in an individual baking dish. Spoon one-fourth of the cheese mixture over each patty. Brown the remaining patties lightly in the skillet. Stack on top of the cheese patties. Divide the remaining cheese mixture over the ground beef stacks. Bake in a preheated 375-degree oven for 20 to 30 minutes or until the patties are cooked through. Each stack may be topped with onion slices or bell pepper rings prior to baking.

Serves 2

Asian Pork Tenderloin

1/4 cup orange juice	1 tablespoon brown sugar
4 garlic cloves, minced	1 tablespoon sesame oil
2 teaspoons fresh ginger, minced	1 tablespoon sesame seeds, toasted
3 tablespoons soy sauce	2 pounds pork tenderloin
1 tablespoon rice wine vinegar	1/4 cup bourbon (optional)

Combine the orange juice, garlic, ginger, soy sauce, vinegar, brown sugar, sesame oil and sesame seeds in a bowl and mix well. Place the tenderloin in a sealable plastic bag. Pour the marinade over the tenderloin and seal the bag. Marinate in the refrigerator for 8 to 10 hours. Drain the tenderloin, reserving the marinade. Place the tenderloin on a rack in a roasting pan. Bake in a preheated 350-degree oven for 30 minutes per pound or until cooked through, basting every 10 minutes with the reserved marinade. Remove from the oven and cut into slices. Place on a flameproof platter. Warm the bourbon in a saucepan. Carefully ignite and pour over the tenderloin. Serve while still flaming.

Serves 4 to 6

Mustard Pork Tenderloin

2 1/4 pounds pork tenderloin

1/2 teaspoon pepper

1 1/4 cups dry white wine

1 cup chicken broth

2 tablespoons coarse-grain mustard

1 tablespoon chopped fresh thyme

1 teaspoon minced garlic

1 tablespoon olive oil

1 1/2 teaspoons kosher salt

1/2 teaspoon pepper

1/2 cup all-purpose flour

Remove the silver skin from the tenderloin, leaving a thin layer of fat. Place the tenderloin and 1/2 teaspoon pepper in a sealable plastic bag. Mix the wine, broth, mustard, thyme and garlic in a bowl. Pour over the tenderloin and seal the bag. Marinate in the refrigerator for 24 hours, turning occasionally. Drain the tenderloin, discarding the marinade.

Pat the tenderloin dry and coat evenly with the olive oil. Sprinkle evenly with the salt and 1/2 teaspoon pepper. Dredge in the flour. Place on a lightly greased rack in a broiler pan. Broil 5 1/2 inches from the heat source for 27 to 30 minutes or until brown and 150 degrees on a meat thermometer, turning occasionally. Let stand for 10 minutes before serving.

Serves 6 to 8

Cuba Libre Pork Chops

¼ cup dark rum   ¼ cup kosher salt

1 (12-ounce) can cola   ¼ cup honey

Zest and juice of 2 limes   4 pork chops

¼ cup packed brown sugar

Combine the rum, cola, lime zest, lime juice, brown sugar, salt and honey in a bowl and mix well. Place the pork chops in a sealable plastic bag. Add the marinade and seal the bag. Marinate in the refrigerator for 4 hours or up to 2 days. Drain the pork chops, discarding the marinade. Place the pork chops in a baking dish. Bake in a preheated 350-degree oven for 30 to 35 minutes or until cooked through and the juices run clear. Serve with plantains and black beans with rice.

Serves 4

Pineapple Pork Chops and Rice

4 to 6 slices pineapple   2 tablespoons butter

16 to 24 whole cloves   1 cup uncooked rice

4 to 6 pork chops   2½ cups chicken broth

Seasoned salt to taste   1 teaspoon salt

½ green bell pepper, chopped   Pinch of thyme

1 large onion, chopped   2 to 3 teaspoons brown sugar

2 ribs celery, chopped   2 to 3 teaspoons butter

Drain the pineapple, reserving the juice. Stud each pineapple slice with four cloves. Drizzle with the reserved pineapple juice and let stand at room temperature. Sprinkle the pork chops with seasoned salt. Brown the pork chops in a skillet and set aside. Sauté the bell pepper, onion and celery in 2 tablespoons butter in a skillet until tender. Add the rice. Cook until golden brown, stirring constantly. Stir in the broth, 1 teaspoon salt and the thyme. Bring to a boil. Pour into a 9×13-inch baking dish. Arrange the pork chops over the rice mixture. Bake, covered, in a preheated 350-degree oven for 1 hour. Remove from the oven. Place one prepared pineapple slice over each pork chop. Sprinkle ½ teaspoon brown sugar over each. Top each with ½ teaspoon butter and spoon the reserved pineapple juice over the top. Bake, uncovered, for 15 minutes. Serve immediately.

Serves 4 to 6

Drunken Pork Stew

2 large dried chipotle chiles

2 large dried ancho chiles

1 (12-ounce) bottle Mexican beer

1/4 cup white or silver tequila

3 1/2 pounds pork shoulder

2 teaspoons kosher salt

1 tablespoon vegetable oil

1 onion, chopped

3 garlic cloves, chopped

12 ounces tomatoes, chopped

2 teaspoons Mexican oregano

2 teaspoons ground cumin

Wipe the chiles clean with a damp cloth. Toast the chiles in a dry heavy saucepan over medium heat for 3 to 5 minutes or until fragrant and puffy, turning occasionally to prevent burning. Let cool slightly. Remove the stems, seeds and membranes. Place the chiles in a saucepan. Add the beer and tequila. Let stand until softened.

Cut the pork into 2-inch pieces. Sprinkle with the salt. Heat the oil in a Dutch oven over medium to high heat. Brown the pork one-half at a time in the hot oil for 8 to 10 minutes per batch, turning frequently. Remove the pork to a bowl. Add the onion and garlic to the pan drippings. Cook for 5 minutes or until tender, stirring frequently. Stir in the chile mixture, tomatoes, oregano, cumin and pork. Add water if needed to barely cover the pork. Bring to a boil over high heat. Bake, covered, in a preheated 350-degree oven for 3 hours or until the pork falls apart. Skim the fat from the surface and remove the chiles. Ladle into serving bowls. Garnish with cojitia cheese and serve with tortilla chips and lime wedges.

Serves 6

Classic Lasagna

12 ounces mild Italian sausage, casings removed
12 ounces ground beef
Salt and pepper to taste
1 (48-ounce) jar meat-flavored spaghetti sauce
12 ounces ricotta cheese
1 egg, lightly beaten
1/2 cup (2 ounces) shredded Parmesan cheese
1 cup (4 ounces) shredded Gruyère cheese
1 cup (4 ounces) shredded Swiss cheese
1 cup (4 ounces) shredded Cheddar cheese
2 cups (8 ounces) shredded mozzarella cheese
8 ounces cream cheese, softened
3/4 cup sour cream
16 ounces no-cook lasagna noodles

Brown the sausage and ground beef in a large skillet, stirring until crumbly; drain. Sprinkle with salt and pepper. Stir in the spaghetti sauce. Bring to a boil. Reduce the heat and simmer for 15 minutes; set aside.

Mix the ricotta cheese, egg and Parmesan cheese in a small bowl. Mix the Gruyère cheese, Swiss cheese, Cheddar cheese and 1 cup of the mozzarella cheese in a medium bowl. Beat the cream cheese and sour cream in a small bowl until smooth.

Spread a thin layer of the meat sauce in a 9×13-inch baking dish. Alternate layers of the noodles, ricotta cheese mixture, Gruyère cheese mixture, cream cheese mixture and the remaining meat sauce in the prepared dish, ending with a layer of noodles and meat sauce. Bake in a preheated 350-degree oven for 20 to 25 minutes or until heated through. Sprinkle with the remaining 1 cup mozzarella cheese. Bake for 10 to 15 minutes longer. Let stand for 15 minutes before serving.

Serves 6

Bella Pasta

3 cups penne

4 ounces cream cheese

1 cup milk

1/4 cup (1 ounce) grated
Parmesan cheese

6 slices bacon, crisp-cooked
and crumbled

2 cups baby spinach leaves

1/3 cup chopped drained oil-pack
sun-dried tomatoes

1 teaspoon Italian seasoning

Cook the pasta using the package directions. Cook the cream cheese, milk and Parmesan cheese in a large saucepan over medium-high heat until smooth, stirring frequently. Add the bacon, spinach, sun-dried tomatoes and Italian seasoning. Cook until heated through, stirring constantly. Drain the pasta. Add to the sauce and toss to coat.

Serves 4

Pasta Maria

8 ounces bacon, chopped

4 ounces prosciutto, thinly sliced
and chopped

1/2 cup thinly sliced sweet onion

3 garlic cloves, finely chopped

1 teaspoon coarsely ground pepper

3 tablespoons extra-virgin olive oil

1 cup mushrooms, sliced

1 cup steamed fresh asparagus pieces

1/2 cup fresh or frozen peas

3 tablespoons butter

1/4 cup half-and-half

6 cups whole wheat pasta, cooked
and drained

Cook the bacon and prosciutto in a 12-inch skillet over medium-high heat until almost crisp; drain. Add the onion, garlic, pepper and olive oil. Cook over medium heat until the onion is tender and translucent. Add the mushrooms, asparagus, peas and butter. Cook until the vegetables are heated through and well coated, stirring constantly. Stir in the half-and-half. Cook until heated through. Pour over the pasta and toss to coat. Serve with freshly grated Parmesan cheese, a mixed green salad and fresh Italian bread.

Serves 6

Lamb Chops
with Jalapeño Mint Sauce

4 medium loin lamb chops

1 tablespoon all-purpose flour

1 tablespoon spicy steak seasoning

1 tablespoon olive oil

1/2 cup low-sodium chicken broth

1/2 cup jalapeño jelly

1 small jalapeño chile, seeded and sliced

2 tablespoons chopped fresh mint

Trim any fat from the lamb chops. Mix the flour and steak seasoning together. Dredge the lamb chops in the flour mixture. Heat the olive oil in a sauté pan over medium-high heat. Add the lamb chops. Sear for 5 minutes on each side for medium-rare. Remove the lamb chops to a platter and keep warm.

Add the broth to the pan drippings, stirring to scrape up any brown bits from the bottom of the pan. Add the jelly and jalapeño chile. Bring to a boil. Cook until the jelly melts, stirring constantly. Reduce the heat. Simmer for 3 minutes. Remove from the heat. Stir in the mint. Drizzle about 3 tablespoons of the sauce over each lamb chop and serve.

Serves 4

Buffalo Meat Loaf

1 cup chopped onion

1 tablespoon chopped garlic

2 teaspoons vegetable oil

3/4 cup fine bread crumbs

1/2 cup chopped fresh flat-leaf parsley

1 egg, lightly beaten

2 tablespoons ketchup

1 tablespoon Worcestershire sauce

2 teaspoons salt

1/4 teaspoon pepper

13/4 pounds ground buffalo

6 shallots, cut into 1/3-inch wedges

6 plum tomatoes, each cut into 6 wedges

1 teaspoon vegetable oil

Salt and pepper to taste

1/3 cup water

Sauté the onion and garlic in 2 teaspoons oil in a large nonstick skillet over medium heat until the onion is softened. Combine with the bread crumbs, parsley, egg, ketchup, Worcestershire sauce, 2 teaspoons salt and 1/4 teaspoon pepper in a large bowl and mix well. Stir in the buffalo. Do not overmix. Shape into a 4×10-inch oval loaf and place in a large shallow metal baking pan.

Toss the shallots and tomatoes with 1 teaspoon oil and salt and pepper to taste. Scatter around the meat loaf and add the water. Bake on the middle oven rack in a preheated 375-degree oven for 1 hour and 10 minutes or until 160 degrees on a meat thermometer. Remove the meat loaf and vegetables to a serving platter. Let stand for 10 minutes before serving.

Serves 6

RANCHING

Ranching in Galveston County was an integral part of the economy. It began in the late 1800s with Anglo-American cattleman settling the land. The ranchers used Spanish and Celtic ranching methods to raise their herd and cattle. The mineral-rich soil and abundance of marshes and wetlands provided ideal conditions for growing crops and kept the cattle fed and healthy. Today there are still many sustainable ranches and farms around the county.

Texas Two Step

A Menu for a Romantic Dinner for Two

Appetizer
Artichoke Croustades 41

Salad
Roquefort Pear Salad 62

Entrée
Filets Mignons with Cabernet Sauce 102

Side Dishes
Horseradish Mashed Potatoes 152
Lemon-Roasted Vegetables 158

Dessert
Triple Layer Chocolate Cheesecake 168

Catch of the Coast

SEAFOOD

Being surrounded by water provides our residents with opportunities not available to those further inland. Our ship channels, ports, and harbors are essential to our economy. Places like the Port of Galveston bring cruise ships and tourists while the Texas City Dike offers a fishing pier for locals.

Just taking a drive around Galveston County will lend pictures of piers, Seaport Museums, lighthouses, and grand sailing ships. The *Elissa*, also known as the "Tall Ship of Texas," is a national historic landmark, and to see her nineteen sails is to be in awe of boats that once were.

Whether you are in search of a catch of the coast or just want to walk down to Pier 21 for dinner with a view, Galveston's seafood will have you hook, line and sinker.

Saltwater Grill

sponsor

Pier 19 was designated as an entertainment sector of the port in 1977 to house boat slips, docks for shrimp and party boats, retail outlets, and restaurants. The Mosquito Fleet is where the shrimp boats would tie up to the pier and sort their catch. Katie's Seafood Market offers the freshest catch of the day. They sell a variety of fish, shrimp, fresh oysters, and crab. The Ocean Star is an offshore drilling rig and museum where tourists can actually step foot on a real offshore rig.

Galveston Crab Cakes

1 pound fresh lump crab meat
3/4 cup Italian bread crumbs
1 egg, beaten
1/4 cup good-quality mayonnaise
1 teaspoon Worcestershire sauce
1 teaspoon dry mustard
1/2 teaspoon salt
1/4 teaspoon pepper
1/2 teaspoon parsley
Vegetable oil for frying

Place the crab meat in a large bowl and carefully remove any shells. Add the bread crumbs and mix gently. Beat the egg, mayonnaise, Worcestershire sauce, dry mustard, salt, pepper and parsley in a bowl until combined. Add to the crab meat mixture and mix gently. Shape into six patties. Fry in hot oil in a large skillet for 3 minutes on each side or until golden brown. Serve with lemon wedges.

Serves 6

Crab Meat au Gratin

1/4 cup (1/2 stick) butter

1 teaspoon minced fresh garlic

1/4 cup sifted all-purpose flour

1 3/4 cups milk

1/8 teaspoon freshly ground pepper

1/2 teaspoon sea salt

1/4 cup marsala

1/2 cup (2 ounces) shredded Cheddar cheese

1/2 cup (2 ounces) shredded Romano cheese

1 pound white crab meat

1 tablespoon chopped fresh parsley

1/2 cup Italian bread crumbs

2 tablespoons butter

Hot cooked rice or toast points

Melt 1/4 cup butter in a medium saucepan. Add the garlic and sauté just until tender. Add the flour gradually, stirring constantly. The mixture will be very thick. Stir in the milk gradually. Cook until thickened and smooth, stirring constantly. Stir in the pepper, salt and wine. Remove from the heat. Add the Cheddar cheese and Romano cheese and stir until melted and smooth. Stir in the crab meat and parsley gently. Spoon into a lightly greased 8×8-inch baking dish.

Sauté the bread crumbs in 2 tablespoons butter in a skillet until the butter is completely absorbed and the mixture is crumbly. Sprinkle over the crab meat mixture. Bake in a preheated 400-degree oven for 10 to 15 minutes or until bubbly and light brown on top. Let stand for 10 minutes before serving. Serve over hot cooked rice or toast points.

Serves 6

Crab Meat Enchiladas

1 (8-ounce) jar green taco sauce
1/2 cup sour cream
8 flour or corn tortillas
8 ounces Monterey Jack
cheese, shredded

1 1/2 cups fresh crab meat
1/2 cup chopped green onions
1 1/2 cups small curd cottage cheese
2 tablespoons skim milk
2 teaspoons chopped garlic

*B*lend the taco sauce and sour cream in a bowl. Spread 1 tablespoon of the taco sauce mixture on each tortilla. Top with the cheese, crab meat and green onions. Roll up to enclose the fillings. Spoon the remaining taco sauce mixture in a greased 7×12-inch baking pan. Place the enchiladas seam side down in the sauce. Process the cottage cheese, milk and garlic in a food processor until smooth. Pour over the enchiladas. Bake in a preheated 375-degree oven for 25 minutes or until hot and bubbly. Garnish with chopped black olives and additional green onions.

Serves 8

Crayfish Fettuccini

1 white onion, chopped
1 bell pepper, chopped
2 garlic cloves, minced
1/2 cup (1 stick) butter
1 pound crayfish tails
4 cups (1 quart) half-and-half

8 ounces Velveeta cheese
1 teaspoon cayenne pepper
Salt and black pepper to taste
2 (9-ounce) packages refrigerated
   fettuccini

*S*auté the onion, bell pepper and garlic in the butter in a skillet. Stir in the crayfish tails. Add the half-and-half and Velveeta. Cook until the Velveeta melts, stirring constantly. Sir in the cayenne pepper, salt and black pepper. Cook the pasta using the package directions; drain. Add to the crayfish mixture and toss to coat. Spoon into a large baking dish. Bake in a preheated 350-degree oven for 30 minutes or until hot and bubbly. Garnish with 3 tablespoons chopped fresh parsley

Serves 6

Bacon and Leek Oysters

1 tablespoon butter
1 tablespoon all-purpose flour
1 cup whipping cream
8 ounces applewood-smoked bacon
4 cups thinly sliced leeks
1 cup finely chopped celery
1 bay leaf
1/8 teaspoon cayenne pepper
2 tablespoons dry white wine
2 tablespoons grated Romano cheese
1/4 teaspoon each salt and pepper
20 medium fresh oysters, shucked
1 cup bread crumbs

Melt the butter in a small skillet over medium heat. Whisk in the flour. Cook for 2 minutes, whisking constantly. Whisk in the cream gradually. Cook until slightly thickened, whisking constantly. Remove from the heat.

Sauté the bacon in a large heavy skillet over medium heat for 6 minutes or until crisp. Remove to paper towels to drain. Crumble the bacon. Drain the bacon drippings, reserving 2 tablespoons in the skillet. Add the leeks, celery, bay leaf and cayenne pepper. Sauté over medium heat for 12 minutes or until the vegetables are tender. Add the wine. Cook for 15 seconds or until the wine is absorbed. Add the cream mixture. Bring to a simmer. Cook for 3 minutes or until slightly thickened, stirring constantly. Stir in the bacon, cheese, salt and pepper. Cool slightly. Discard the bay leaf.

Place one oyster on each of twenty oyster shells or place two oysters in each of ten small ramekins. Top each oyster with 2 tablespoons of the leek mixture or top the oysters in the ramekins with 1/4 cup of the leek mixture. Place on a rimmed baking sheet. Sprinkle with the bread crumbs. Bake in a preheated 500-degree oven for 8 minutes or until the edges of the oysters curl, the mixture bubbles and the bread crumbs are golden brown.

Serves 10

ELISSA

The Elissa is a three-masted sailing ship that was built in 1877 in Scotland. It is a National Historic Landmark, and recognized as one of the finest ship restorations in the world. It is famously also known as the "Tall Ship of Texas." The Elissa has 19 sails, measures 99 feet high, and weighs 620 tons. It is presently kept at the Texas Seaport Museum on Pier 21 in Galveston.

Bourbon Bacon Scallops

3 tablespoons minced green onions
2 tablespoons bourbon
2 tablespoons pure maple syrup
1 tablespoon soy sauce

1 tablespoon Dijon mustard
1/4 teaspoon pepper
24 large sea scallops
6 slices bacon

Combine the green onions, bourbon, maple syrup, soy sauce, Dijon mustard and pepper in a large bowl and mix well. Add the scallops and stir gently to coat. Marinate, covered, in the refrigerator for 1 hour, stirring occasionally. Drain the scallops, reserving the marinade. Cut each bacon slice into four equal pieces. Wrap each scallop with a piece of bacon. Thread the scallops onto four 12-inch skewers, leaving some space between each so the bacon can cook. Place on a rack in a broiler pan coated with nonstick cooking spray. Broil for 8 minutes or until the bacon is crisp and the scallops are opaque and slightly firm, basting occasionally with the reserved marinade.

Serves 4

Creamy Basil Scallops

1/4 cup (1/2 stick) butter
12 sea scallops
Salt and ground black pepper to taste
2 tablespoons butter
1/4 cup chopped shallots
1 teaspoon slivered garlic

Pinch of crushed red pepper
1/2 cup dry white wine
3/4 cup heavy cream
10 basil leaves, cut into thin ribbons
Hot cooked pasta

Heat 1/4 cup butter in a skillet over medium-high heat. Add the scallops after the foam subsides. Sprinkle with salt and black pepper. Brown for 2 to 3 minutes on each side, adjusting the heat as needed. Remove from the heat. Place the scallops on a plate and set aside. Cool the skillet and wipe with a paper towel to clean. Melt 2 tablespoons butter in the skillet over medium heat. Add the shallots, garlic, red pepper, salt and black pepper. Cook for 2 minutes or until the shallots are tender. Add the wine and increase the heat. Simmer for 1 minute or until the mixture is reduced by about half. Add the cream. Cook until the mixture is reduced by about half. Add the scallops and accumulated juices. Cook for 1 minute. Add one-half of the basil. Cook until the scallops are opaque and slightly firm. Adjust the seasonings to taste. Serve over pasta and sprinkle with the remaining basil.

Serves 4

Garlic Baked Shrimp

1 1/4 pounds medium shrimp, peeled and deveined

1/2 cup Italian bread crumbs

3 tablespoons finely chopped fresh parsley

1 teaspoon grated fresh lemon zest

1/4 teaspoon salt

3 garlic cloves, minced

2 tablespoons fresh lemon juice

4 teaspoons olive oil

Place the shrimp in a baking dish coated with nonstick cooking spray. Mix the bread crumbs, parsley, lemon zest, salt and garlic in a bowl. Stir in the lemon juice and olive oil. Sprinkle over the shrimp. Bake in a preheated 400-degree oven for 13 minutes or until the shrimp turn pink and the bread crumbs are light brown.

Serves 4

Spicy Shrimp with Walnuts

1/2 cup soy sauce

1/2 cup vegetable oil

1/2 cup dry sherry

2 tablespoons dark sesame oil

1 1/2 tablespoons sugar

8 small dried chiles, or to taste

2 tablespoons minced garlic

2 to 3 tablespoons minced fresh ginger

3 pounds large shrimp, peeled and deveined

1 1/2 bunches green onions

1 cup walnut halves

Peanut oil or other cooking oil

Hot cooked rice

Combine the soy sauce, vegetable oil, sherry, sesame oil, sugar, dried chiles, garlic and ginger in a large bowl and mix well. Add the shrimp and toss to coat. Marinate, covered, in the refrigerator for 1 to 2 hours. Cut the green onions diagonally into 1 1/2-inch pieces and chill. Toast the walnuts on a baking sheet in a preheated 250-degree oven for 15 minutes, watching carefully to prevent burning. Remove from the oven to cool.

Place enough peanut oil in a large wok or skillet to coat and heat over medium heat. Drain the shrimp, reserving the marinade. Add the shrimp to the peanut oil. Stir-fry for 2 to 3 minutes or until the shrimp curl and turn pink. Remove with a slotted spoon to a warm serving platter. Pour the reserved marinade and walnuts into any accumulated juices in the wok. Cook over medium-high heat until the liquid is reduced to a syrup, stirring constantly. Return the shrimp to the wok. Add the green onions and stir to coat with the sauce. Serve immediately over rice.

Serves 6

Shrimp Étouffée

3 tablespoons butter

1 tablespoon olive oil

2 tablespoons all-purpose flour

1/3 cup finely chopped onion

2 ribs celery, finely chopped

1/2 bell pepper, finely chopped

1 jalapeño chile, seeded and chopped

3 garlic cloves, finely chopped

1 cup chicken broth

1/2 cup white wine

1 tablespoon Old Bay seasoning or other Creole seasoning

1 tablespoon chopped fresh parsley

1 teaspoon Worcestershire sauce

1 teaspoon hot pepper sauce

Salt and pepper to taste

1 pound shrimp, peeled and deveined

4 cups cooked rice

Melt the butter with the olive oil in a large skillet over medium-high heat. Add the flour. Cook until thickened, stirring constantly. Add the onion, celery, bell pepper and jalapeño chile. Cook until softened, stirring constantly. Add the garlic. Cook for 1 minute, stirring constantly. Stir in the broth, wine, Old Bay seasoning, parsley, Worcestershire sauce, hot sauce, salt and pepper. Reduce the heat to a simmer. Add the shrimp. Cook for 5 minutes or until the shrimp turn pink, turning once. Pour over the cooked rice in a serving bowl. Serve with garlic bread and a salad.

Serves 4

Shrimp and Oyster Gumbo

6 tablespoons all-purpose flour

5 tablespoons bacon drippings

2 onions, chopped

1 cup chopped celery

2 garlic cloves, minced

1 (28-ounce) can chopped tomatoes

1 (6-ounce) can tomato sauce

5 cups water

1 cup chicken broth

2 or 3 whole crabs, cleaned

1 tablespoon salt

1 teaspoon ground pepper

2 teaspoons Creole seasoning

Hot pepper sauce to taste

3 bay leaves

1 (16-ounce) package frozen okra

4 pounds (16- to 20-count) shrimp, peeled and deveined

1 pint oysters

Gumbo filé to taste

Hot cooked rice

Mix the flour and bacon drippings in a large heavy stockpot. Cook over medium heat for 30 minutes to form a very dark roux, stirring constantly. Add the onions, celery and garlic and sauté for 7 minutes. Add the tomatoes, tomato sauce, water, broth, crabs, salt, pepper, Creole seasoning, hot sauce and bay leaves. Bring to a boil. Reduce the heat and simmer for 1 hour. Add the okra. Continue to cook over low heat for 1 1/2 hours. Add the shrimp and oysters. Cook for 15 minutes or until the shrimp turn pink. Add filé powder. Discard the bay leaves. Ladle over hot rice in serving bowls. This recipe may be prepared in advance, chilled and reheated before serving. If oysters are not in season, leave them out or substitute 1 pound crab claw meat. The gumbo will still be flavorful.

Serves 12

PORT OF GALVESTON

The Port of Galveston is the oldest port in the Gulf of Mexico west of New Orleans. It began as a trading post in 1825 and was formally established by the Congress of Mexico. By 1900 the port was leading the country in cotton exportation and third for wheat. It was once home port for the Texas Navy and has since played an integral role in the production and exportation of Imperial Sugar. Presently, the port is home to numerous cruise ships.

Dill Shrimp Pasta

8 ounces angel hair pasta

1 cup (2 sticks) butter

1 1/2 pounds peeled medium shrimp

4 garlic cloves, minced

2 cups half-and-half

1/2 cup chopped fresh parsley

1/2 teaspoon salt

1/2 teaspoon pepper

2 teaspoons chopped fresh dill weed, or

3/4 teaspoon dried dill weed

Cook the pasta using the package directions. Drain and keep warm. Melt the butter in a large heavy skillet over medium-high heat. Add the shrimp and garlic. Cook for 3 to 5 minutes or until the shrimp turn pink, stirring constantly. Remove the shrimp with a slotted spoon to a bowl. Pour the half-and-half into the drippings in the skillet. Bring to a boil, stirring gently. Reduce the heat. Simmer for 15 minutes or until thickened, stirring occasionally. Return the shrimp to the skillet. Stir in the parsley, salt, pepper and dill weed. Spoon over the hot pasta. Garnish with sprigs of fresh dill weed.

Serves 6

Greek Shrimp Linguini

8 ounces linguini

5 or 6 scallions

1/4 cup olive oil

2 pounds shrimp, peeled and deveined

1 cup white wine

1 teaspoon dry mustard

1/3 teaspoon red pepper flakes

3/4 cup chopped parsley

1/2 cup fish stock or water

1 tablespoon lemon juice

3/4 cup crumbled feta cheese

Salt and pepper to taste

Cook the pasta using the package directions. Drain and cool. Sauté the scallions in the olive oil in a skillet until tender. Add the shrimp, wine, dry mustard, red pepper flakes, parsley, stock and lemon juice. Cook for 5 minutes or until the shrimp turn pink. Drain and cool. Add the cheese and toss to mix. Pour over the linguini and serve at room temperature.

Serves 8

Grilled Marinated Calamari

2 pounds cleaned calamari tubes and tentacles
1 tablespoon minced garlic
1¹/₂ teaspoons red chile flakes
¹/₄ cup chopped flat-leaf parsley
¹/₃ cup extra-virgin olive oil
2 tablespoons fresh lemon juice
¹/₂ teaspoon sea salt
¹/₃ cup extra-virgin olive oil
2 tablespoons fresh lemon juice
¹/₂ teaspoon sea salt

Combine the calamari, garlic, chile flakes, parsley, ¹/₃ cup olive oil, 2 tablespoons lemon juice and ¹/₂ teaspoon sea salt in a medium bowl and mix well. Marinate in the refrigerator for 1 to 5 hours, stirring frequently. Pour into a colander to drain. Separate the calamari tubes and tentacles.

Place the calamari tubes on a grill rack. Grill over high heat for 3 minutes or just until firm, turning once. Drop the tentacles into clumps on the grill rack using tongs. Grill until the tentacles firm up and then spread out evenly to grill. The total grilling time for the tentacles will be 4 minutes. Place the calamari tubes and tentacles in a serving dish. Drizzle with ¹/₃ cup olive oil and 2 tablespoons lemon juice. Sprinkle with ¹/₂ teaspoon sea salt.

Serves 4

Stuffed Gulf Coast Flounder

1/2 cup chopped green onions

1/2 cup chopped celery

1/2 cup chopped bell pepper

2 or 3 tablespoons olive oil

2 garlic cloves, minced

8 ounces lump crab meat

8 ounces shrimp or crayfish, peeled

3 tablespoons minced fresh parsley

3/4 to 1 cup bread crumbs

1 egg, beaten

Salt, black pepper and cayenne pepper to taste

2 to 4 pounds flounder, each butterflied with skin on

1 bottle white wine

Sauté the green onions, celery and bell pepper in the olive oil in a skillet. Add the garlic and sauté until the vegetables are soft. Add the crab meat, shrimp, parsley and 3/4 cup bread crumbs. Remove from the heat to cool. Stir in the egg. Add salt, black pepper and cayenne pepper. Add the remaining bread crumbs if the mixture is too moist. Stuff the flounder with the seafood mixture. Place each stuffed flounder in a foil pocket filled with 1/2 cup wine. Do not seal the top. Place on a grill rack. Grill for 20 minutes or until the fish flakes easily. The stuffed flounder may be placed with a small amount of wine in a glass baking dish and baked in a preheated 375-degree oven for 20 to 25 minutes or until the fish flakes easily.

Serves 4

Grouper with Roasted Corn and Red Bell Pepper

1 large red bell pepper, cut into 1/2-inch chunks	1/4 teaspoon dried thyme
	1 tablespoon vegetable oil
2 cups fresh corn kernels	2 pounds grouper fillets, cut into 4 pieces
1 tablespoon vegetable oil	1/4 teaspoon salt
1/4 teaspoon salt	1/4 teaspoon pepper
1/4 teaspoon pepper	1/4 teaspoon dried thyme

Combine the bell pepper, corn, 1 tablespoon oil, 1/4 teaspoon salt, 1/4 teaspoon pepper and 1/4 teaspoon thyme in a large roasting pan and mix well. Roast in a preheated 450-degree oven for 12 minutes or until the corn and bell pepper begin to brown, stirring twice. Rub 1 tablespoon oil over each side of the fish. Sprinkle with 1/4 teaspoon salt, 1/4 teaspoon pepper and 1/4 teaspoon thyme. Remove the roasting pan from the oven. Push the corn mixture to the sides of the pan. Place the fish skin side down in the center of the pan. Bake for 15 minutes or until the fish flakes easily. Serve with the roasted corn and bell pepper.

Serves 4

Salmon with Fresh Tomato-Basil Relish

1 pound Campari or Roma tomatoes, seeded and chopped	1/4 teaspoon coarsely ground pepper
	4 (6-ounce) salmon fillets
1/2 cup thinly sliced fresh basil	1/2 teaspoon ground cumin
2 garlic cloves, minced	3/4 teaspoon salt
2 tablespoons balsamic vinegar	1/4 teaspoon coarsely ground pepper
3/4 teaspoon salt	1 teaspoon olive oil

Combine the tomatoes, basil, garlic, vinegar, 3/4 teaspoon salt and 1/4 teaspoon pepper in a small bowl and mix well. Chill until serving time. Sprinkle the fish with the cumin, 3/4 teaspoon salt and 1/4 teaspoon pepper. Heat the olive oil in a large nonstick skillet over medium-high heat. Add the fish skin side down. Cook for 4 minutes. Turn and cook for 1 minute longer. Reduce the heat to medium. Cook, covered, for 2 to 3 minutes or until the fish is opaque in the center and flakes easily. Place the fish on serving plates and top with the cold relish. Serve immediately.

Serves 4

Sesame Salmon

1/4 cup soy sauce
2 tablespoons dry sherry
1/4 cup chicken broth
1/2 teaspoon sugar
1 1/2 teaspoons grated fresh ginger
1 garlic clove, minced
2 teaspoons cornstarch
3 tablespoons water
1 egg white
2 tablespoons cornstarch
1 (2-pound) salmon fillet, cut into 4 pieces
1/4 cup sesame seeds
1/4 cup vegetable oil

Combine the soy sauce, sherry, broth, sugar, ginger and garlic in a small bowl and mix well. Dissolve 2 teaspoons cornstarch in the water in a small bowl. Whisk the egg white and 2 tablespoons cornstarch in a bowl. Brush the skinless side of the salmon with the egg white mixture. Dip in the sesame seeds to coat.

Heat the oil in a large nonstick skillet over medium-high heat. Place the salmon in the hot oil sesame seed side down. Cook for 5 minutes or until golden brown. Turn and cook for 3 minutes longer or until the salmon flakes easily. Remove from the skillet and keep warm. Drain any pan drippings from the skillet.

Pour the soy sauce mixture into the skillet. Simmer for 2 minutes, stirring constantly. Whisk in the cornstarch mixture. Cook for 1 minute or until thickened, stirring constantly. Serve the salmon with the sauce poured around it.

Serves 4

Pier 21 is part of the Port of
Galveston. It is located on 21st Street
and Harborside. Pier 21 is home to a
variety of wonderful tourist attractions.
The Texas Seaport Museum educates
visitors about Galveston immigration
and port commerce. The Elissa,
known as "the official tall ship of
Texas," is a three-masted sailing
vessel located at Pier 21. The 1900
Great Storm Theatre recounts the
nation's worst natural disaster
in a one-hour documentary. The
Seagull II is available for harbor
tours and dolphin watching.

Stuffed Red Snapper

8 ounces fresh mushrooms
2 tablespoons butter
1/2 cup finely chopped celery
3 tablespoons minced onion
1/2 cup soft bread crumbs
1 egg, lightly beaten
1 tablespoon soy sauce
1 tablespoon chopped fresh flat-leaf parsley
Salt and pepper to taste
2 (2 1/2-pound) oven-ready whole red snappers,
scaled and cleaned
2 tablespoons butter
2 tablespoons minced onion
1/2 cup dry white wine
3/4 cup water

Clean the mushrooms and pat dry. Chop one-half of the mushrooms
finely. Cut the remaining mushrooms into quarters. Melt 2 tablespoons
butter in a skillet. Add the celery and 3 tablespoons onion. Sauté for
5 minutes. Combine the sautéed mixture with the mushrooms, bread
crumbs, egg, soy sauce, parsley, salt and pepper in a bowl and mix
well. Spoon into the fish cavities and secure with skewers or wooden
picks. Sprinkle both sides of the stuffed fish with salt and pepper. Place
in a large baking dish. Top with 2 tablespoons butter, 2 tablespoons
onion, the wine and water. Bake in a preheated 350-degree oven for
45 to 50 minutes or until the fish flakes easily, basting occasionally with
the pan juices.

Serves 4

Citrus Tilapia

Orange Ginger Sauce

1/4 cup orange marmalade

1/4 cup orange juice

2 tablespoons rice vinegar

1 tablespoon minced fresh ginger

1/2 teaspoon red pepper flakes

1 teaspoon minced garlic

1 tablespoon vegetable oil

Salt and pepper to taste

Fish

1/2 teaspoon Chinese five-spice powder

1/4 teaspoon salt

1/4 teaspoon cayenne pepper

2 tablespoons vegetable oil

4 to 6 tilapia fillets

1 tablespoon vegetable oil

2 tablespoons minced scallions

To prepare the sauce, whisk the marmalade, orange juice, vinegar, ginger and red pepper flakes in a bowl. Sauté the garlic in the oil in a small skillet over medium to high heat for 30 seconds. Add the marmalade mixture. Simmer for 5 minutes or until thickened, stirring constantly. Add salt and pepper.

To prepare the fish, mix the Chinese five-spice power, salt and cayenne pepper with 2 tablespoon oil in a bowl. Pat the fish dry with a paper towel. Brush both sides with the spice mixture. Heat 1 tablespoon oil in a skillet over medium-high heat until hot. Add the fish. Cook for 3 minutes on each side. Sprinkle with the scallions. Pour the sauce over the fish and serve.

Serves 4

Tuna Alexander

4 mushrooms, chopped
1 to 2 teaspoons minced fresh garlic
2 tablespoons chopped white onion
1 teaspoon chopped fresh mint
1/2 teaspoon minced fresh ginger
2 teaspoons lime juice
2 tablespoons sesame oil
2 tuna steaks
1 tablespoon tequila
1 tablespoon sake
2 tablespoons oyster sauce
Pepper to taste

Sauté the mushrooms, garlic, onion, mint, ginger and lime juice in the sesame oil in a hot skillet over medium to medium-high heat. Cook for 5 minutes, stirring constantly. Spoon into a bowl and set aside. Place the fish in the skillet. Sear for a few seconds on each side. Return the mushroom mixture to the skillet. Add the tequila and sake and ignite. Flambé for less than 1 minute. Add the oyster sauce during the last few seconds and serve immediately. The fish is supposed to be rare.

Serves 2

Fish Tacos

Creamy Picante Sauce
2 cups sour cream
3/4 cup picante sauce
1 teaspoon ground cumin

Pico de Gallo
2 large tomatoes, seeded and chopped
1/2 cup chopped onion
1/4 cup finely chopped fresh jalapeño chiles
1/4 cup finely chopped cilantro
1 tablespoon fresh lime juice
1 teaspoon salt

Tacos
2 pounds mild white fish, such as tilapia
1/2 cup (1 stick) butter
1 teaspoon ground cumin
1 teaspoon garlic salt
16 corn tortillas

To prepare the sauce, mix the sour cream, picante sauce and cumin in a bowl. Chill until serving time.

To prepare the pico de gallo, combine the tomatoes, onion, jalapeño chiles, cilantro, lime juice and salt in a bowl and mix well. Chill for 1 hour before serving.

To prepare the tacos, place the fish in a single layer on one or two sheets of heavy duty foil. Dot with the butter. Sprinkle with the cumin and garlic salt. Fold the foil to enclose the fish and seal well. Place on a grill rack. Grill over medium heat for 10 minutes or until the fish flakes easily. Heat the tortillas in a microwave or in a small amount of hot oil in a skillet until soft. Fill a doubled tortilla with the fish, sauce and pico de gallo and serve.

Serves 4 to 6

The Texas City Dike is a man-made breakwater built by tumbled granite. It extends about five miles into Galveston Bay and ends near the junction of the Texas City ship channel and Houston ship channel. Its purpose is to reduce the amount of sand drifting into the ship channel. It was authorized as such by the Texas Legislator in 1935. Many locals enjoy the dike by using it as a long fishing pier. Unfortunately, the dike was harmed by Hurricane Ike in 2008.

Hook, Line, and Sinker

A MENU FOR A
SEAFOOD SPREAD FOR FOUR

Appetizer
Southern Shrimp Rémoulade 34

Soup
Oyster Rockefeller Soup 56

Entrée
Stuffed Red Snapper 138

Side Dish
Scalloped Potatoes 155

Dessert
Peach Bread Pudding 169

Coastal Complements

VEGETABLES, SIDES

Many think of Galveston and immediately think of the coast when in fact, our culture would not be what it is without our surrounding cities.

Dickinson, which hosts railroad and oil industries, is a city situated between Houston and Galveston. Texas City, which began as a series of small settlements, attracted fisherman and cattle ranchers alike in the 1830s. Here industry is king, and many companies house their refineries, chemical plants, and railroads. Live oak trees define League City, a small town with historic homes, parks, and shops. Take a stroll down Main Street and get a glimpse of Americana as it was years ago.

Still have a thirst for the water? Kemah may be just your style. With a name meaning "wind in my face," this town of two thousand residents enjoys a boardwalk and amusement park, all fit for a boater's delight.

Galveston's surrounding cities bring the inland flair and keep us anchored. We hope these vegetables and side dishes will do the same, adding Coastal Complements to any of your meals.

Sky Bar

sponsor

Asian Asparagus Bundles

1 pound sliced bacon, cut into halves
1 to 2 pounds asparagus, trimmed
1/2 cup (1 stick) butter

1/4 cup packed brown sugar
3 tablespoons soy sauce
2 garlic cloves, minced

Wrap one piece of bacon around each asparagus spear. Place seam side down in a 9 · 13-inch baking dish. Heat the butter, brown sugar, soy sauce and garlic in a saucepan just until bubbly. Pour over the asparagus bundles. Marinate, covered with plastic wrap, in the refrigerator for 1 to 10 hours. Bake, uncovered, in a preheated 350-degree oven for 20 minutes or until the bacon is crisp. Broil for 2 to 3 minutes longer for crispier bacon. Serve hot.

Serves 6

Boraccho Beans

2 cups dried pinto beans
5 cups water
Salt to taste
1 pound sliced bacon, chopped
1 onion, chopped

4 large tomatoes, chopped
3 serranos, chopped
4 garlic cloves, minced
1/2 bunch cilantro, chopped

Sort and rinse the beans. Place in a large saucepan and add water to cover. Boil for 2 minutes. Cover and remove from the heat. Let stand for 2 hours. Drain the beans and return to the saucepan. Add 5 cups water and salt. Bring to a boil; reduce the heat. Simmer for 2 hours, adding additional water as needed to keep the beans covered. Cook the bacon in a deep skillet until crisp; drain. Add the onion, tomatoes, chiles, garlic and cilantro. Sauté until the onion is translucent. Add to the beans. Simmer for 1 hour. Garnish with additional cilantro.

Serves 6

Green Bean Bunches

1 to 1 1/2 pounds fresh green beans
1 large bunch scallions
2 cups all-purpose flour

3 tablespoons Jane's Krazy Mixed-up Salt, or other salt-based seasoning blend
4 cups vegetable oil
1 1/2 cups buttermilk

Trim the green beans and cut into 2-inch pieces. Remove the white portions of the scallions and reserve for another purpose. Cut the scallion stems down the center to make two long strips if the stems are very thick. Sift the flour with the Mixed-up Salt. Tie four or five green beans with a scallion stem to form a bundle, wrapping the scallion around the green beans more than once before tying. Repeat with the remaining green beans and scallion stems. Heat the oil in a deep-fryer or skillet. Dip each green bean bundle into the buttermilk and coat with the flour mixture. Fry in the hot oil until golden brown. Remove to paper towels to drain. Serve immediately. You may add a slice of bacon or a bell pepper strip to the green bean bundles for a change of taste.

Serves 8

Green Bean Toss

2 cups fresh or frozen green beans
1 tablespoon olive oil
1/2 cup walnuts
1/4 cup crumbled feta cheese

1 cup grape tomatoes, sliced lengthwise
1/2 cup vinaigrette
Salt and pepper to taste

Cook the green beans in water in a saucepan for 8 to 10 minutes or until al dente. Plunge into ice water to stop the cooking process. Heat the olive oil in a skillet over high heat. Add the walnuts and sauté until golden brown. Drain the green beans. Combine the green beans, walnuts, cheese and tomatoes in a bowl. Add the vinaigrette and toss to coat. Sprinkle with salt and pepper.

Serves 6

Broccoli Parmesan Casserole

The Bolivar Lighthouse was built in 1872 to guide ships through the channel from the Gulf of Mexico into the Port of Galveston. It was constructed 117 feet above sea level and composed of brick and cast-iron plates. It withstood both the 1900 and 1915 hurricanes and suffered only minor damage from Hurricane Ike. In 1933 the Lighthouse was retired and replaced by the South Jetty light. It was sold to a private owner and is not open to the public.

8 cups coarsely chopped broccoli florets
1/3 cup all-purpose flour
1/4 teaspoon salt
1/4 teaspoon dry mustard
1 1/2 cups milk
1 cup chicken broth
1 cup (4 ounces) shredded extra-sharp Cheddar cheese
6 tablespoons grated Parmesan cheese
2 tablespoons diced pimentos, drained
1/4 teaspoon pepper
12 pieces garlic melba toast rounds
2 tablespoons grated Parmesan cheese

Cook the broccoli in boiling water in a saucepan for 3 minutes or until tender-crisp; drain. Mix the flour, salt and dry mustard in a large heavy saucepan. Whisk in the milk and broth. Cook over medium heat for 8 minutes or until thickened, stirring constantly. Remove from the heat. Add the Cheddar cheese and 6 tablespoons Parmesan cheese and stir until melted. Stir in the pimentos and pepper. Add the broccoli and toss to coat. Spoon into a 9 · 13-inch baking dish coated with nonstick cooking spray.

Pulse the toast rounds in a food processor ten times or until coarse crumbs form and measure 1 cup. Mix the coarse crumbs with 2 tablespoons Parmesan cheese. Sprinkle over the broccoli mixture. Spray the top lightly with nonstick cooking spray. Bake in a preheated 400-degree oven for 15 minutes or until bubbly. Let stand for 5 minutes before serving.

Serves 8

Breaded Brussels Sprouts

1½ pounds brussels sprouts	¼ cup dry bread crumbs
1 teaspoon salt	¼ teaspoon garlic powder
2 tablespoons butter, melted	¼ teaspoon pepper
¼ cup (1 ounce) grated	¼ teaspoon salt
Parmesan cheese	2 tablespoons butter, melted

Rinse and trim the brussels sprouts; remove the stems. Place the brussels sprouts in a medium saucepan and cover with water. Add 1 teaspoon salt. Bring to a boil; reduce the heat. Simmer, covered, for 6 minutes or until tender; drain. Do not overcook. Add 2 tablespoons butter and toss to coat. Place in a small baking dish.

Mix the cheese, bread crumbs, garlic powder, pepper, ¼ teaspoon salt and 2 tablespoons butter in a bowl. Sprinkle over the brussels sprouts. Broil 4 inches from the heat source for 5 minutes or until the crumb mixture is light brown. Serve hot.

Serves 12

Honey-Glazed Carrots

Salt to taste	1 tablespoon fresh lemon juice
1 pound baby carrots	½ teaspoon pepper
2 tablespoons butter	¼ cup chopped flat-leaf parsley
2 tablespoons honey	

Bring water to a boil in a medium saucepan. Add salt and carrots. Cook for 5 to 6 minutes or until the carrots are tender. Drain the carrots and return to the saucepan. Add the butter, honey and lemon juice. Cook for 5 minutes or until the carrots are glazed. Add salt and pepper. Sprinkle with the parsley.

Serves 4

Cheesy Cream Corn with Cilantro

TEXAS CORINTHIAN YACHT CLUB

The Texas Corinthian Yacht Club is located in Kemah, Texas, and was established in 1937. This yacht club was created by four local families who wanted to promote amateur sailing in the area. Presently the land includes a large area of water for races as well as a family-friendly clubhouse surrounded by cabanas. TCYC offers sailing instruction programs for all age groups and is home to many races throughout the year.

12 medium ears of corn
3 tablespoons unsalted butter
1 1/2 cups chopped scallions
1/2 teaspoon salt
1/2 teaspoon pepper
2/3 cup heavy cream
2 tablespoons cornstarch
1 large garlic clove
6 ounces queso fresco, crumbled
1 cup cilantro sprigs

Remove the husks and silk from the corn. Cut the kernels into a bowl using a sharp knife. Heat the butter in a deep 12-inch heavy skillet over medium-high heat until the foam subsides. Add the scallions. Cook for 5 minutes or until softened, stirring occasionally. Add the corn, salt and pepper. Cook for 5 minutes, stirring occasionally.

Blend the cream and cornstarch in a small bowl. Stir into the corn mixture. Simmer for 3 minutes or until slightly thickened, stirring constantly. Purée 1 1/2 cups of the corn mixture with the garlic in a blender. Return to the skillet. Cook until heated through, stirring constantly. Spoon into a serving bowl. Sprinkle with the queso fresco and cilantro.

Serves 6

Eggplant Parmesan

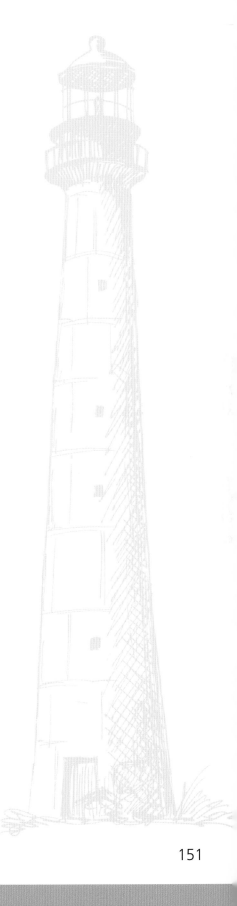

1¹⁄₂ cups chopped onions

12 garlic cloves, minced

¹⁄₂ tablespoon red pepper flakes

¹⁄₄ cup extra-virgin olive oil

3 (28-ounce) cans crushed tomatoes

24 fresh basil leaves, coarsely chopped

¹⁄₂ teaspoon dried oregano

2 teaspoons salt

2 eggplant

2 eggs

1 cup milk

3 cups Italian bread crumbs

¹⁄₂ cup extra-virgin olive oil

12 ounces mozzarella cheese, shredded

Sauté the onions, garlic and red pepper flakes in ¹⁄₄ cup olive oil in a saucepan over medium-high heat for 5 minutes. Reduce the heat to low. Cook for 10 minutes longer. Add the tomatoes, basil, oregano and salt. Simmer for 30 minutes.

Peel the eggplant and cut into ¹⁄₂-inch-thick slices. Beat the eggs with the milk in a shallow dish. Dip the eggplant into the egg mixture and then into the bread crumbs. Repeat the process. Brown the eggplant on each side in ¹⁄₂ cup olive in a skillet.

Pour one-fourth of the sauce in a large baking dish. Layer the eggplant in the sauce. Cover with as much of the remaining sauce as desired. Bake in a preheated 350-degree oven for 30 to 45 minutes or until heated through and bubbly. Cover the top with the cheese. Bake until the cheese melts.

Serves 6

Miso-Glazed Eggplant

4 Japanese eggplant

3 tablespoons vegetable oil

1/3 cup yellow or red miso

2 tablespoons light brown sugar

2 tablespoons sake or white wine

1/4 teaspoon red chile flakes

1/4 cup cilantro leaves

1 teaspoon sesame seeds, toasted

Cut the eggplant into halves lengthwise. Score the cut side of the eggplant 1/4 inch deep. Heat the oil in an ovenproof skillet over high heat. Add the eggplant scored side down. Cook for 4 minutes or until softened and brown. Mix the miso, brown sugar, sake and chile flakes in a small bowl. Turn the eggplant and brush with the miso mixture. Broil 4 inches from the heat source for 3 minutes or until the glaze begins to brown. Sprinkle with the cilantro and sesame seeds.

Serves 4

Horseradish Mashed Potatoes

4 pounds gold creamer potatoes

2 bay leaves

2 tablespoons salt

2 cups sour cream

1/2 cup (1 stick) unsalted butter

3 tablespoons horseradish

1/4 teaspoon salt

1/4 teaspoon pepper

3 tablespoons chopped fresh chives

Peel the potatoes. Cut into large pieces and place in a large saucepan. Cover with water. Add the bay leaves and 2 tablespoons salt. Bring to a boil over medium-high heat. Cook for 20 minutes or until tender. Remove the bay leaves. Drain the potatoes, reserving 2 tablespoons of the cooking liquid. Mash the potatoes with the reserved liquid in a large mixing bowl. Add the sour cream, butter, horseradish, 1/4 teaspoon salt and the pepper and mix well. Spoon into a serving bowl and sprinkle with the chives.

Serves 6

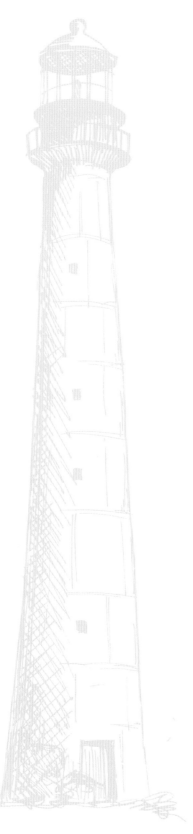

Wasabi Mashed Potatoes

2½ pounds Idaho potatoes
⅓ teaspoon salt
⅓ cup cream
1½ tablespoons wasabi paste

Peel the potatoes. Cut the potatoes into chunks and place in a saucepan. Cover with water and bring to a boil. Add the salt. Cook for 10 to 12 minutes or until tender. Drain the potatoes and return to the saucepan. Add the cream and wasabi paste. Mash with a potato masher until the desired consistency.

Serves 6

Mashed Potato Patties

4 cups mashed cooked potatoes
1 onion, chopped
1 teaspoon minced garlic
1 red bell pepper, minced
1 egg
1 cup (4 ounces) shredded Cheddar cheese
1½ cups all-purpose flour
1 tablespoon butter
Salt and pepper to taste

Combine the mashed potatoes, onion, garlic, bell pepper, egg and cheese in a bowl and mix well. Shape into large balls. Roll in the flour and then flatten into patties ½ to ¾ inch thick. Melt the butter in a skillet over medium to high heat. Add the patties. Cook for 5 minutes on each side or until brown. Sprinkle with salt and pepper.

Serves 8

Scalloped Potatoes

2 tablespoons unsalted butter
1 large shallot, finely chopped
1 garlic clove, minced
1/4 teaspoon crushed red pepper
2 pounds red potatoes, peeled and
   cut into 1/8-inch slices
1 3/4 cups heavy cream

1 1/2 cups milk
1/2 teaspoon salt
1/4 teaspoon pepper
1/2 cup (2 ounces) shredded
   Gruyère cheese
2 tablespoons grated Parmesan cheese

Melt the butter in a saucepan over low heat. Add the shallot and sauté for 1 minute. Add the garlic and red pepper. Cook for 3 minutes or until softened. Add the potatoes and toss lightly. Pour in the cream, milk, salt and pepper. Bring to a boil, stirring occasionally. Remove from the heat. Spoon into a buttered baking dish. Sprinkle with the Gruyère cheese and Parmesan cheese. Bake in a preheated 375-degree oven for 15 minutes. Reduce the oven temperature to 350 degrees. Bake for 45 minutes longer or until bubbly and golden brown.

Serves 6

Whipped Sweet Potatoes

8 medium sweet potatoes
1 cup evaporated milk
2 teaspoons vanilla extract
1/2 cup packed brown sugar
1/4 cup granulated sugar
1/4 cup (1/2 stick) butter

2 tablespoons orange juice
1/2 teaspoon cinnamon
Pinch of nutmeg
1 cup chopped pecans
4 pears, peeled, poached and puréed

Bake the sweet potatoes in a preheated 400-degree oven for 45 to 60 minutes or until tender. Reduce the oven temperature to 350 degrees. Peel the sweet potatoes. Beat the sweet potatoes in a bowl until smooth. Scald the evaporated milk, vanilla, brown sugar, granulated sugar and butter in a saucepan. Add to the sweet potatoes and mix well. Add the orange juice, cinnamon, nutmeg, pecans and pear purée and mix well. Pour into a baking dish. Bake for 15 minutes or until heated through.

Serves 8 to 10

Mashed Butternut Squash

League City is located between

Houston and Galveston and has the

charm of a small town with easy

access to big city attractions. It was

named after J.C. League, a Galveston

entrepreneur who purchased the

cattle ranching town. The beauty of

League City is defined by its huge

one-hundred-year old live oak trees,

restored historic homes, green parks,

and quaint antique shops. Main

Street offers its visitors a variety of

boutiques and restaurants.

1 large butternut squash (about 1 pound)
2 Anjou pears
1/4 cup (1/2 stick) unsalted butter
1 small vanilla bean
1 tablespoon brown sugar
2 teaspoons ginger
1/2 teaspoon salt, or to taste
1/2 teaspoon pepper, or to taste

Cut the butternut squash into halves lengthwise and remove the seeds. Peel the pears. Cut the pears into halves and remove the core. Place the squash and pears cut side up on a foil-lined baking sheet.

Melt the butter in a small saucepan over low heat. Cut the vanilla bean into halves lengthwise and scrape the seeds of each side with a paring knife. Add the seeds to the butter. Reserve the pod for another use. Whisk the brown sugar and ginger into the butter mixture. Remove from the heat. Brush onto the cut sides of the squash and pears. Sprinkle with 1/2 teaspoon salt and 1/2 teaspoon pepper. Set the remaining butter mixture aside and keep warm.

Roast the squash and pears in a preheated 375-degree oven for 45 to 60 minutes or until a knife can be inserted easily into the squash. Scoop the inside of the squash into a large bowl, discarding the skin. Add the pears and mash with a fork or potato masher. Stir in the remaining butter mixture. Sprinkle with salt and pepper to taste.

Serves 4

Zucchini Bake

2 tablespoons butter

1 onion, chopped

1 garlic clove, minced

3 or 4 zucchini and/or yellow squash, cut into 1-inch slices

3 large tomatoes, cut into small pieces

3/4 cup Italian bread crumbs

1 teaspoon salt

1/2 teaspoon pepper

1 teaspoon dried basil

8 ounces Swiss cheese, cut into small chunks

1/4 cup Italian bread crumbs

4 ounces Swiss cheese, shredded

Melt the butter in a large sauté pan. Add the onion, garlic and zucchini. Sauté until the onion is translucent, stirring frequently. The zucchini should stay firm. Combine the zucchini mixture, tomatoes, 3/4 cup bread crumbs, the salt, pepper, basil and cheese chunks and mix lightly. Spoon into a 2-quart baking dish sprayed with nonstick cooking spray. Sprinkle with 1/4 cup bread crumbs and the shredded cheese. Bake in a preheated 375-degree oven for 30 to 40 minutes or until heated through. Using a mixture of zucchini and yellow squash adds color and flavor.

Serves 6 to 8

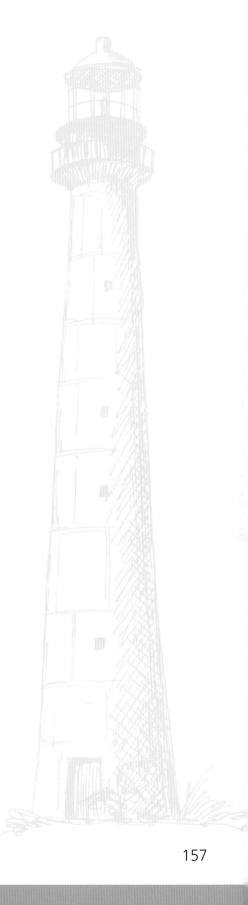

South Shore Skillet Spinach

2 tablespoons butter
1 tablespoon all-purpose flour
1 tablespoon grated onion
2 cups frozen or cooked fresh spinach
3 eggs, lightly beaten

1/3 cup (2 ounces) shredded
  Cheddar cheese
Salt and pepper to taste
1 garlic clove, pressed

Melt the butter in a skillet. Stir in the flour and onion. Cook over medium heat for 5 minutes or until light brown. Stir in the spinach. Cook until heated through, stirring constantly. Stir in the eggs. Add the cheese, salt, pepper and garlic. Cook for 5 minutes or until the eggs are set and the cheese is melted.

Serves 6

Lemon-Roasted Vegetables

2 tablespoons olive oil
1 tablespoon fresh lemon juice
1 garlic clove, minced
1/2 teaspoon salt
1 large red bell pepper, cut into
  1-inch pieces

1 large yellow squash, cut into
  1-inch pieces
1 large zucchini, cut into 1-inch pieces
1 tablespoon chopped fresh basil
1/3 cup sliced almonds, toasted

Combine the olive oil, lemon juice, garlic and salt in a bowl and mix well. Add the bell pepper, squash and zucchini and toss to coat. Place in a single layer in a foil-lined 10 · 15-inch baking pan. Bake in a preheated 400-degree oven for 10 minutes. Stir the vegetables. Bake for 10 minutes longer or until tender. Place in a large serving dish. Add the basil and toss to mix. Sprinkle with the almonds.

Serves 4

Red Wine-Poached Pears

2 cups dry red wine
1 navel orange, peeled and quartered
1 1/2 cups sugar
1 (4-inch) stick cinnamon, broken into halves
6 whole cloves
2 cups water
2 Bartlett pears, peeled, cored and cut into halves
1/4 cup mascarpone cheese
1/4 cup heavy whipping cream
2 tablespoons sugar

Bring the wine, orange, 1 1/2 cups sugar, the cinnamon, cloves and water to a boil in a 4-quart saucepan over high heat. Add the pears and reduce the heat to a simmer. Place a plate on top of the pears to submerge them in the liquid. Cook, covered, for 15 minutes or until tender when pierced with a fork.

Whisk the mascarpone cheese, cream and 2 tablespoons sugar in a small bowl until very thick. Place the pear halves in shallow serving bowls with 1/4 cup of the poaching liquid. Dollop with the cheese mixture.

Serves 4

Breaded Risotto Cakes

1/2 tablespoon kosher salt

1 cup arborio rice

2 extra-large eggs

3 tablespoons minced fresh chives

1 1/2 cups shredded Italian fontina cheese

1 tablespoon minced garlic

1 1/4 teaspoons kosher salt

1/2 teaspoon pepper

3/4 cup panko (Japanese bread crumbs)

3 tablespoons (or more) olive oil

*B*ring a large saucepan of water to a boil over medium-low heat. Add 1/2 tablespoon salt and the rice. Cook for 20 minutes or until the rice grains are soft, stirring occasionally. Drain the rice in a fine mesh sieve and rinse under cold water until cool. Drain well.

Whisk the eggs, chives, cheese, garlic, 1 1/4 teaspoons salt and the pepper in a medium bowl. Add the cooled rice and mix well. Chill, covered with plastic wrap, for 2 to 10 hours or until firm.

Spread the panko in a shallow dish. Heat the olive oil in a large skillet over medium-low heat. Shape the rice mixture into balls using a large spoon. Pat the rice balls into cakes 3 inches in diameter and 3/4 inch thick. Place four to six cakes in the panko, turning once to coat. Fry the cakes in the hot oil for 3 minutes on each side or until crisp and brown, turning once. Place on a baking sheet lined with baking parchment and keep warm in a preheated 250-degree oven for up to 30 minutes. Repeat with the remaining cakes in batches, adding additional olive oil as needed.

Serves 6

The city of Dickinson is situated between Houston and Galveston. It is originally named after John Dickinson, who in 1824 purchased the land known as Dickinson today. By 1860 Dickinson had become a stop on the Galveston, Houston, and Henderson Railroad. Its economy was sustained by the quality of soil and its ability to grow fruit, cane, berries, and potatoes. The railroad, oil industry, and establishment of NASA all contributed to sustain Dickinson's economy.

Wild Rice Salad

Parmesan Vinaigrette

1 cup canola oil

1/4 cup white vinegar

1/4 cup (1 ounce) grated
Parmesan cheese

3/4 teaspoon sugar

1 teaspoon salt

1 teaspoon celery seeds

1/2 teaspoon dry mustard

1/4 teaspoon paprika

1 garlic clove, minced

Salad

1 (6-ounce) jar marinated artichoke hearts

2 cups water

1/2 teaspoon salt

1 cup wild rice

6 ounces frozen green peas

1/3 cup coarsely chopped green
bell pepper

3 green onions, chopped

1 cup cherry or grape tomatoes,
cut into halves

1/4 cup slivered almonds, toasted

1/4 cup sliced black olives

To prepare the vinaigrette, combine the canola oil, vinegar, cheese, sugar, salt, celery seeds, dry mustard, paprika and garlic in a jar with a tight-fitting lid. Seal the lid and shake well to mix. Chill until serving time.

To prepare the salad, drain the artichoke hearts, reserving the marinade. Cut the artichoke hearts into halves. Bring the water and salt to a boil in a 1-quart saucepan. Stir in the rice. Reduce the heat to low. Simmer, covered, for 45 to 60 minutes or until tender. Drain the excess liquid from the rice. Combine the rice, artichoke hearts, peas, bell pepper, green onions, tomatoes, reserved marinade and one-half of the vinaigrette in a large bowl and toss well. Chill, covered, or serve at room temperature. Toss again just before serving, adding some of the remaining vinaigrette, if desired. Sprinkle with the slivered almonds and black olives and serve.

Serves 8

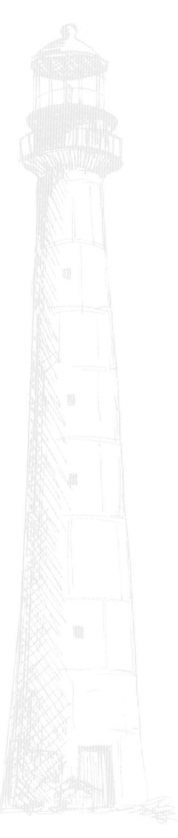

Baked Cheese Grits

5 cups chicken broth

1 1/4 cups quick-cooking grits

1 cup (4 ounces) shredded extra-sharp Cheddar cheese

1 cup (4 ounces) shredded Monterey Jack cheese

1/4 cup whipping cream

1 teaspoon hot pepper sauce

1/4 teaspoon black pepper

1/4 teaspoon red pepper

1 teaspoon Worcestershire sauce

3 eggs, lightly beaten

Bring the broth to a boil in a medium saucepan over medium-high heat. Whisk in the grits gradually. Return to a boil. Reduce the heat to medium-low and simmer for 10 minutes or until thickened, stirring occasionally. Stir in the Cheddar cheese, Monterey Jack cheese, whipping cream, hot sauce, black pepper, red pepper and Worcestershire sauce. Cook until the cheeses melt, stirring constantly. Remove from the heat. Stir a small amount of the hot grits into the beaten eggs. Stir the eggs into the hot grits. Pour into a lightly greased 2-quart or 8 · 11-inch baking dish. Bake, uncovered, in a preheated 350-degree oven for 40 to 45 minutes or until golden brown and set.

Serves 6 to 8

Macaroni and Cheese

1/2 cup (1 stick) butter
1/2 cup all-purpose flour
2 cups milk
2 bay leaves
1 tablespoon Worcestershire sauce
1/2 teaspoon nutmeg
1/2 teaspoon cayenne pepper
1/2 teaspoon dry mustard
1/2 cup (2 ounces) shredded white Cheddar cheese
1/2 cup (2 ounces) shredded Monterey Jack cheese
1/2 cup (2 ounces) shredded Asiago cheese
1 cup finely chopped ham
1 pound rotini, cooked and drained
2 tablespoons chili powder

Melt the butter in a medium saucepan over medium heat. Stir in the flour. Add the milk. Bring to a simmer, stirring frequently. Add the bay leaves, Worcestershire sauce, nutmeg, cayenne pepper and dry mustard and mix well. Add the Cheddar cheese, Monterey Jack cheese and Asiago cheese. Continue to heat until the cheeses are melted and blended into the sauce, stirring frequently. Stir in the ham. Remove the bay leaves. Pour the sauce over the pasta in a large bowl and toss to coat. Spread evenly into a large buttered baking dish. Sprinkle with the chili powder. Bake for 35 minutes or until hot and bubbly.

Serves 8

KEMAH, TEXAS

Kemah, Texas, was established in 1898 under its original name of Evergreen. In 1907 a request for a post office was denied because there was already a town named Evergreen. The citizens changed the name to Kemah, which is an Indian word meaning "wind in my face." Today Kemah has more than two thousand residents and is home to the family-friendly Kemah Boardwalk, which is an amusement park with a variety of restaurants.

Oldies, But Goodies

A Menu for Family Comfort Food

Appetizer
Sicilian Stuffed Mushrooms 42

Salad
Caesar Salad 64

Entrée
Southern Garlic Fried Chicken 85

Side Dishes
South Shore Skillet Spinach 158
Macaroni and Cheese 163

Dessert
Fresh Apple Cake 177

Lasting Impressions

DESSERTS

We've taken a journey through Galveston's culture, making many stops along the way. Great places would be nothing without great foundations. Galveston County, with its buildings and structures rich in history, is no different.

Take a stroll along the Galveston Historic Homes Tour, ending with the Annual Linen and Lace Mother's Day Brunch, and you'll see life here is pretty sweet. Our homes have seen hurricanes, economic changes, and wars, and have survived to tell stories about each. Tickle your inner adventurer and go explore the Bishop's Palace or Moody Mansion. Looking for something more spiritual? Perhaps one of our old churches would be a good stop. Sacred Heart Catholic Church has survived two major hurricanes and still has its original stained glass windows.

The historical structures of Galveston are certain to make a lasting impression, and so will these desserts. Grab a map and your sense of exploration, and of course, something to satisfy your sweet tooth.

HOTEL GALVEZ & SPA
A Wyndham Grand Hotel

sponsor

Triple Layer Chocolate Cheesecake

Cheesecake

1 (8-ounce) package chocolate wafer cookies, crushed (about 2 cups)

1/4 cup granulated sugar

5 tablespoons butter, melted

8 ounces cream cheese, softened

1/4 cup granulated sugar

1 egg

1/4 teaspoon vanilla extract

2 ounces semisweet chocolate, melted

1/3 cup sour cream

8 ounces cream cheese, softened

1/3 cup packed dark brown sugar

1 tablespoon all-purpose flour

1 egg

1/2 teaspoon vanilla extract

1/4 cup chopped pecans

5 ounces cream cheese, softened

1/4 cup granulated sugar

1 egg

1 cup sour cream

1/4 teaspoon vanilla extract

1/4 teaspoon almond extract

Chocolate Glaze

6 ounces semisweet chocolate

1/4 cup (1/2 stick) butter or margarine

3/4 cup sifted confectioners' sugar

2 tablespoons water

1 teaspoon vanilla extract

To prepare the cheesecake, combine the cookie crumbs, 1/4 cup granulated sugar and the butter in a medium bowl and mix well. Press over the bottom and 2 inches up the side of a 9-inch springform pan. Beat 8 ounces cream cheese and 1/4 cup granulated sugar in a mixing bowl until fluffy. Add 1 egg and 1/4 teaspoon vanilla and mix well. Stir in the chocolate and 1/3 cup sour cream. Spoon over the chocolate crust. Beat 8 ounces cream cheese, the brown sugar and flour in a mixing bowl until fluffy. Add 1 egg and 1/2 teaspoon vanilla and mix well. Stir in the pecans. Spoon gently over the chocolate layer. Beat 5 ounces cream cheese and 1/4 cup granulated sugar in a mixing bowl until fluffy. Add 1 egg and beat well. Stir in 1 cup sour cream, 1/4 teaspoon vanilla and the almond extract. Spoon gently over the pecan layer. Bake in a preheated 325-degree oven for 1 hour. Turn off the oven. Let stand in the closed oven for 30 minutes. Open the oven door and let stand for 30 minutes longer. Remove from the oven to cool. Chill for 8 hours.

To prepare the glaze, melt the chocolate and butter in a double boiler over hot water, stirring frequently. Remove from the heat. Stir in the confectioners' sugar, water and vanilla until smooth.

To serve, release the cheesecake from the side of the pan and remove. Spread the warm glaze over the cheesecake.

Serves 12

Peach Bread Pudding

4 cups cubed French bread

3 eggs, beaten

2 cups milk

1/2 cup granulated sugar

1/2 teaspoon almond extract

1 (21-ounce) can peach pie filling

2 tablespoons brown sugar

1/2 teaspoon cinnamon

2 tablespoons sliced almonds

1 tablespoon butter

Spread the bread cubes in a 7×11-inch baking pan sprayed with nonstick cooking spray. Whisk the eggs, milk, granulated sugar and almond extract in a bowl. Stir in the pie filling. Pour over the bread cubes and press into the bread with the back of a spoon. Sprinkle a mixture of the brown sugar and cinnamon over the peach mixture. Top with the almonds and dot with the butter. Bake in a preheated 350-degree oven for 50 to 55 minutes or until a knife inserted in the center comes out nearly clean. Serve warm with ice cream. Cover and chill any remaining bread pudding for up to 3 days.

Serves 8

Blackberry Crisp

1 cup all-purpose flour

1 cup sugar

1 teaspoon baking powder

1 egg, beaten

2 tablespoons all-purpose flour

3/4 cup sugar

4 to 5 cups fresh or frozen blackberries

2 tablespoons cornstarch

1/2 cup (1 stick) unsalted butter, melted

Mix 1 cup flour, 1 cup sugar and the baking powder in a bowl and make a well in the center. Add the egg to the well and mix until crumbly. Mix 2 tablespoons flour and 3/4 cup sugar in a small bowl. Toss the blackberries with the cornstarch in a large bowl. Add the sugar mixture and toss gently to coat. Spoon into a buttered oval baking dish. Spread the crumbled topping over the top. Drizzle with the butter. Place on a baking sheet to prevent bubbling over onto your oven. Bake in a preheated 375-degree oven for 45 minutes.

Serves 8

The Galveston Historic Foundation preserves and restores a variety of buildings and houses around Galveston. Every year during the first two weekends in May, they showcase a number of these historically significant landmarks through a homes tour. Tourists can visit the houses on the tour at their own pace and admire the beauty that each offers. The Annual Linen and Lace Mother's Day Brunch is an added bonus to the festivities.

Key Lime Bites

1 1/3 cups graham cracker crumbs
1/3 cup sugar
1/4 cup (1/2 stick) butter, melted
4 egg yolks
1 egg
1 (14-ounce) can sweetened condensed milk
1/4 cup lemon juice
1/4 cup Key lime juice

Mix the graham cracker crumbs, sugar and butter in a bowl. Place a small spoonful of the buttered crumbs in the bottom of each paper-lined miniature muffin cup and press over the bottom and part way up the side. Bake in a preheated 350-degree oven for 3 to 5 minutes or until set. Remove from the oven to cool. Maintain the oven temperature.

Beat the egg yolks, egg, condensed milk, lemon juice and lime juice in a mixing bowl until smooth. Fill each cooled cup with the filling. Bake for 7 minutes or until bubbles appear on the top. Do not overbake, or the texture will be grainy. Remove from the oven to cool. Chill until serving time. Garnish with whipped cream before serving. This recipe may be made as a pie by lining a 9-inch pie plate with the crumb mixture and baking for 15 minutes. Fill with the filling and bake for 15 minutes longer.

Makes 35 to 40 bites

McLeod Crowd Crepes

Crepes

3/4 cup milk

3/4 cup cold water

3 egg yolks

1 tablespoon sugar

3 tablespoons rum

1 1/2 cups all-purpose flour

5 tablespoons butter, melted

Custard

1 egg

1 egg yolk

3/4 cup sugar

1/2 cup all-purpose flour

1 cup boiling milk

3 tablespoons butter

2 teaspoons vanilla extract

1/4 teaspoon almond extract

1/2 cup sliced almonds

2 ounces semisweet chocolate

2 tablespoons butter, melted

1 tablespoon sugar

*T*o **prepare the crepes,** process the milk, water, egg yolks, sugar, rum, flour and 3 1/2 tablespoons of the butter in a blender for 1 minute. Refrigerate for at least 2 hours. Heat a small amount of the remaining butter in a greased crepe pan until sizzling. Ladle 2 tablespoons of the batter into the skillet, tilting to coat evenly. Cook for 15 seconds or until the edge begins to curl from the pan. Turn and cook for 10 seconds or until light brown. Slide onto a plate. Repeat the process with the remaining batter, adding the remaining butter as needed and stacking the crepes between sheets of waxed paper as they are cooked.

To prepare the custard, beat the egg and egg yolk in a mixing bowl until blended. Add 3/4 cup sugar gradually, beating constantly. Beat in the flour and boiling milk. Pour into a double boiler. Cook over hot water until thickened, stirring constantly. Remove from the heat and beat until smooth with an electric mixer. Add 3 tablespoons butter, the vanilla, almond extract and almonds and mix well. Spread 2 tablespoons of the custard on each crepe. Roll up and place in a buttered baking dish. Grate the chocolate over the crepes. Top with 2 tablespoons melted butter and sprinkle with 1 tablespoon sugar. Bake in a preheated 350-degree oven until the chocolate melts. Serve topped with whipped cream, if desired.

Serves 12

Pecan Meringue Pie

2/3 cup shortening
2 cups sifted all-purpose flour
1 tablespoon salt
6 tablespoons cold water
1 cup pecan pieces
1 teaspoon salt
1 teaspoon butter
1 cup sugar
1/4 cup sifted all-purpose flour
1 cup half-and-half
3 egg yolks, lightly beaten
1 to 2 teaspoons vanilla extract
3 egg whites, at room temperature
1/4 teaspoon cream of tartar
1 teaspoon vanilla extract
3 to 4 tablespoons sugar

Cut the shortening into 2 cups flour in a bowl with a pastry blender until crumbly. Dissolve 1 tablespoon salt in the cold water in a small bowl. Add to the flour mixture and mix to form a soft ball of dough. Divide the dough into two equal portions. Roll one portion on a lightly floured surface into a 10-inch circle. Fit in a 9-inch pie plate, fluting the edge. Repeat with the remaining dough and reserve for another pie.

Cook the pecans and 1 teaspoon salt in the butter in a nonstick skillet until the pecans are toasted, stirring frequently. Mix 1 cup sugar, 1/4 cup flour, the half-and-half and egg yolks in a double boiler. Cook over hot water for 35 minutes or until thickened, stirring frequently. Add 1 to 2 teaspoons vanilla and the toasted pecans and mix well. Pour into the pastry-lined pie plate. Beat the egg whites with the cream of tartar in a bowl until soft peaks form. Add 1 teaspoon vanilla. Add 3 to 4 tablespoons sugar gradually, beating constantly until stiff peaks form. Spread over the filling, sealing to the edge. Bake in a preheated 350-degree oven for 15 minutes or until brown.

Serves 6 to 8

A la Crate's Italian Crème Cake

Cake
1/2 cup (1 stick) butter, softened
1/2 cup shortening
2 cups sugar
5 egg yolks
2 cups all-purpose flour, sifted
1 teaspoon baking soda
1/4 teaspoon salt
1 cup buttermilk
2 teaspoons vanilla extract
5 egg whites, stiffly beaten
2 cups shredded coconut
1 cup chopped pecans

Cream Cheese Frosting
16 ounces cream cheese, softened
1 cup (2 sticks) butter, softened
2 teaspoons vanilla extract
2 (1-pound) packages confectioners' sugar, sifted

To prepare the cake, cream the butter, shortening and sugar in a mixing bowl. Add the egg yolks one at a time, beating well after each addition. Add a mixture of the flour, baking soda and salt alternately with the buttermilk and vanilla, beating well after each addition. Fold in the egg whites. Fold in the coconut and pecans. Spoon evenly into three 8-inch cake pans sprayed with nonstick cooking spray. Bake in a preheated 350-degree oven for 25 to 30 minutes or until the layers test done. Cool in the pans for 10 minutes. Invert onto wire racks to cool completely.

To prepare the frosting, beat the cream cheese, butter and vanilla in a mixing bowl until smooth and creamy. Add the confectioners' sugar and beat until smooth. Spread between the layers and over the top and side of the cake.

Serves 12

Brownie Chocolate Cake with Chocolate Buttermilk Frosting

Cake
2 cups all-purpose flour

1 teaspoon baking soda

1/4 cup baking cocoa

1/2 cup buttermilk

1/2 cup sour cream

1 teaspoon vanilla extract

1 cup (2 sticks) butter, softened

2 cups sugar

2 eggs

Chocolate Buttermilk Frosting
1/2 cup (1 stick) butter, softened

1/4 cup baking cocoa, sifted

8 ounces cream cheese, softened

1 (1-pound) package confectioners' sugar

2 tablespoons buttermilk

1 teaspoon vanilla extract

To prepare the cake, grease and flour two 8-inch cake pans and line with baking parchment. Sift the flour, baking soda and baking cocoa together. Whisk the buttermilk, sour cream and vanilla in a small bowl. Cream the butter and sugar in a mixing bowl until light and fluffy. Add the eggs and mix well. Add the flour mixture in three batches alternately with the buttermilk mixture, beating at low speed after each addition. Divide the batter evenly between the prepared cake pans. Bake in a preheated 350-degree oven for 30 to 35 minutes or until a wooden pick inserted in the center comes out clean and the edges of the layers just begin to pull away from the sides of the cake pans. Cool in the cake pans on a wire rack.

To prepare the frosting, beat the butter, baking cocoa and cream cheese at low speed in a mixing bowl until creamy. Beat at high speed until light and fluffy. Reduce the speed to low and add the confectioners' sugar, buttermilk and vanilla. Continue to beat until smooth. Remove the cake layers carefully from the cake pans. Spread the frosting between the layers and over the top and side of the cake.

Serves 10 to 12

Heavenly Chocolate Cake

Cake

2 cups all-purpose flour

2 cups sugar

1 teaspoon baking soda

1 teaspoon cinnamon

1 cup (2 sticks) butter, softened

1 cup water

1/4 cup baking cocoa

2 eggs

1/2 cup buttermilk

1 teaspoon vanilla extract

Chocolate Icing

1/2 cup (1 stick) butter

1/4 cup baking cocoa

6 tablespoons milk

1 (1-pound) package confectioners' sugar

1 teaspoon vanilla extract

1 cup chopped pecans

To prepare the cake, sift the flour, sugar, baking soda and cinnamon together. Simmer the butter, water and baking cocoa in a large saucepan until smooth, stirring frequently. Combine the chocolate mixture with the flour mixture in a large bowl and mix well. Beat the eggs in a bowl. Add the buttermilk and vanilla and mix well. Add to the chocolate batter and mix well. Spoon into a greased 9×13-inch cake pan. Bake in a preheated 350-degree oven for 25 to 30 minutes or until the cake tests done. Remove from the oven to cool slightly.

To prepare the icing, simmer the butter, baking cocoa and milk in a medium saucepan until smooth, stirring frequently. Add the confectioners' sugar and vanilla and mix well. Stir in the pecans. Pour over the warm cake.

Serves 12 to 15

ST. MARY'S MISSION CHURCH

St. Mary's Catholic Church is located in League City, Texas. It is small in size and described as a simple Gothic Revival style church. It was originally built in 1910, and the land was given to the community by Mr. League. He donated it for the construction of a church for the citizens of League City to worship, learn, and play. This church is now designated a historical landmark by the League City Historical Society.

Mexican Chocolate Cake

Cake	Mexican Chocolate Icing
1/2 cup (1 stick) margarine	1/2 cup (1 stick) margarine,
1/2 cup vegetable oil	cut into pieces
2 ounces unsweetened chocolate	2 ounces unsweetened chocolate
1 cup water	6 tablespoons milk
2 cups all-purpose flour	1 (1-pound) package
1 teaspoon baking soda	confectioners' sugar
2 cups sugar	1 teaspoon vanilla extract
1/2 cup buttermilk	1/2 cup chopped pecans (optional)
2 eggs, beaten	
1 teaspoon cinnamon	
1 teaspoon vanilla extract	

To prepare the cake, heat the margarine, oil, chocolate and water in a large saucepan over medium heat until the chocolate is melted. Mix the flour, baking soda, sugar, buttermilk, eggs, cinnamon and vanilla in a large bowl. Add the chocolate mixture and mix with a spoon until blended. Pour into a greased 12×18-inch cake pan. Bake in a preheated 350-degree oven for 20 to 25 minutes or until the cake tests done.

To prepare the icing, heat the margarine, chocolate and milk in a saucepan over medium-high heat until bubbles form around the edge. Remove from the heat. Stir in the confectioners' sugar a small amount at a time. Stir in the vanilla and pecans. Continue to beat until of the desired spreading consistency. Spread over the warm cake.

Sour milk may be used instead of the buttermilk. For 1/2 cup sour milk, place 1 1/2 teaspoons vinegar in a 1-cup measure. Add enough milk to measure 1/2 cup. Let stand for 5 minutes before using. Also, the cake may be baked in a 9×13-inch cake pan and will require a longer baking time.

Serves 15 to 20

Fresh Apple Cake

Cake

2 cups sugar

3 eggs

1 1/2 cups vegetable oil

1/4 cup orange juice

3 cups all-purpose flour

1 teaspoon baking soda

1/4 teaspoon salt

1 tablespoon cinnamon

1 tablespoon vanilla extract

3 cups finely chopped peeled apples

1 cup shredded coconut

1 cup chopped pecans

Fresh Apple Cake Sauce

1/2 cup (1 stick) butter

1 cup sugar

1/2 cup buttermilk

1/2 teaspoon baking soda

To prepare the cake, combine the sugar, eggs, oil, orange juice, flour, baking soda, salt, cinnamon and vanilla in a large bowl and mix well. Fold in the apples, coconut and pecans. Pour into a generously buttered tube pan. Bake in a preheated 325-degree oven for 1 1/2 hours or until the cake tests done.

To prepare the sauce, melt the butter in a large saucepan. Stir in the sugar, buttermilk and baking soda. Bring to a rolling boil, stirring constantly. Boil for 1 minute. Pour the hot sauce over the cake. Let stand for 1 hour. Invert onto a wire rack to cool completely.

Serves 16

Carrot Cake

Cake

2 cups all-purpose flour

2 teaspoons baking powder

1 1/2 teaspoon baking soda

1 1/2 teaspoons salt

2 teaspoons cinnamon

1/2 cup chopped pecans

1/2 cup raisins

2 cups sugar

1 1/4 cups vegetable oil

4 eggs

2 cups finely grated carrots

1 (8-ounce) can crushed pineapple, drained

Cream Cheese Frosting

1/2 cup (1 stick) butter, softened

8 ounces cream cheese, softened

1 teaspoon vanilla extract

1 (1-pound) package confectioners' sugar

To prepare the cake, mix the flour, baking powder, baking soda, salt and cinnamon together. Toss the pecans and raisins with a small amount of the flour mixture to coat and set aside. Combine the sugar, oil and eggs in a mixing bowl and mix well. Add the flour mixture and beat until smooth. Stir in the coated pecans and raisins, carrots and pineapple and mix well. Spoon into two greased and floured 8-inch cake pans. Bake in a preheated 350-degree oven for 30 to 35 minutes or until the layers test done. Cool in the cake pans for 10 minutes. Remove to wire racks to cool completely.

To prepare the frosting, beat the butter, cream cheese, vanilla and confectioners' sugar in a mixing bowl until smooth and creamy. Spread between the layers and over the top and side of the cake.

Serves 10

Harvest Loaf Cake with Spiced Glaze

Cake

1³/4 cups all-purpose flour
1 teaspoon baking soda
1 teaspoon cinnamon
1/2 teaspoon salt
1/2 teaspoon nutmeg
1/4 teaspoon ginger
1/4 teaspoon ground cloves
1/2 cup (1 stick) butter, softened
1 cup sugar
2 eggs

3/4 cup pumpkin purée
1¹/2 cups (9 ounces) semisweet
    chocolate chips
3/4 cup chopped nuts

Spiced Glaze

1/2 cup confectioners' sugar
1/4 teaspoon cinnamon
1/8 teaspoon nutmeg
1 to 2 tablespoons cream

To prepare the cake, fold a piece of waxed paper into thirds and fit down the center of a 5×9-inch loaf pan with the ends extending over the ends of the pan by about 3 inches. Mix the flour, baking soda, cinnamon, salt, nutmeg, ginger and cloves together. Cream the butter and sugar in a mixing bowl until light and fluffy. Beat in the eggs. Add the pumpkin and flour mixture alternately, beating well after each addition. Stir in the chocolate chips and nuts. Spoon into the prepared pan. Bake in a preheated 350-degree oven for 60 to 70 minutes or until the loaf tests done.

To prepare the glaze, combine the confectioners' sugar, cinnamon, nutmeg and cream in a bowl and mix until smooth. Drizzle over the hot cake in the pan. Let stand for 8 to 10 hours. Loosen the edges from the sides of the pan with a knife. Use the waxed paper to lift from the pan so the cake doesn't fall apart. Cut into slices.

Serves 8 to 10

Tres Leches Cake

3 eggs

1 cup sugar

1¹/2 cups all-purpose flour

2 teaspoons baking powder

¹/2 cup milk

2 teaspoons vanilla extract

1 (14-ounce) can sweetened condensed milk

1 (12-ounce) can evaporated milk

¹/2 cup heavy cream

3 egg whites, at room temperature

1 cup sugar

2 teaspoons vanilla extract

Beat the whole eggs in a mixing bowl until foamy. Add 1 cup sugar gradually, beating constantly. Add the flour, baking powder, milk and 2 teaspoons vanilla and mix well. Pour into an ungreased 9×13-inch cake pan. Bake in a preheated 350-degree oven for 20 to 25 minutes or until the cake tests done. Cool in the cake pan.

Poke holes all over the cooled cake with a fork. Blend the condensed milk, evaporated milk and cream in a bowl. Pour over the cake gradually until all of the mixture is absorbed. Beat the egg whites, 1 cup sugar and 2 teaspoons vanilla in a mixing bowl until stiff peaks form. Spread over the cake. Chill until serving time.

For a quicker version, prepare and bake one 2-layer package French vanilla cake mix using the package directions for a 9×13-inch cake pan. Poke holes all over the cooled cake and pour a mixture of one can sweetened condensed milk and one can coconut milk over the top until all of the mixture is absorbed. Frost with whipped topping and chill until serving time.

If you are concerned about using raw egg whites, use whites from eggs pasteurized in their shells, which are sold at some specialty stores, or use an equivalent amount of meringue powder and follow the package directions.

Serves 12

Red Velvet Cake

Cake

1 tablespoon butter
3 1/4 cups cake flour
1 1/2 cups sugar
1 teaspoon baking soda
1 teaspoon baking cocoa
1 teaspoon salt
2 eggs
1 1/2 cups vegetable oil
1 cup buttermilk

2 tablespoons red food coloring
1 teaspoon vanilla extract
1 teaspoon white vinegar

Cream Cheese Frosting

12 ounces cream cheese, softened
1 1/2 cups (3 sticks) butter, softened
1 1/2 teaspoons vanilla extract
3 cups confectioners' sugar
1 1/2 cups chopped pecans

To prepare the cake, grease three 8-inch cake pans with the butter. Sprinkle with 2 tablespoons of the cake flour. Sift the remaining cake flour, sugar, baking soda, baking cocoa and salt together. Beat the eggs, oil, buttermilk, food coloring, vanilla and vinegar in a mixing bowl until blended. Add the cake flour mixture and beat for 1 to 2 minutes or until smooth. Divide the batter evenly among the prepared cake pans. Bake in a preheated 350-degree oven for 25 to 30 minutes or until a wooden pick inserted in the center comes out clean, rotating the cake pans halfway through the baking process. Cool in the cake pans for 5 minutes. Invert each layer onto a plate and then onto a wire rack to cool completely.

To prepare the frosting, beat the cream cheese, butter and vanilla in a mixing bowl until smooth. Add the confectioners' sugar and beat for 5 to 7 minutes or until light and fluffy. Spread the frosting between the layers and over the top and side of the cake. Press the pecans into the side of the cake.

Serves 12

Hotel Galvez's "Pie" in a Pumpkin

8 miniature pumpkins
2 cups apple juice
1 cup canned pumpkin pie filling
1 (4-ounce) package vanilla instant pudding mix
1 teaspoon cinnamon
1/4 teaspoon nutmeg
1/4 teaspoon ginger
1 1/2 cups whipped topping
1 cup graham cracker crumbs
1/4 cup (1/2 stick) butter, melted

Cut the tops from the pumpkins and hollow out the centers. Place the pumpkins in a stockpot. Cover with the apple juice, adding water if needed. Bring to a boil. Remove from the heat. Let stand until the pumpkins are tender. Chill in the refrigerator.

Beat the pumpkin pie filling, pudding mix, cinnamon, nutmeg and ginger at low speed in a mixing bowl for 1 minute. Fold in the whipped topping. Spoon into the pumpkins. Mix the graham cracker crumbs and butter in a bowl. Spoon over the filling before serving.

Serves 8

HOTEL GALVEZ

A group of businessmen pooled their resources after the 1900 Storm and opened the Hotel Galvez in 1911 as a symbol that Galveston had recovered following the devastation of the 1900 Storm. This elegant hotel was immediately proclaimed "Queen of the Gulf." It remains the only historic beachfront hotel on the Texas Gulf Coast and is owned by Galveston preservationists George Mitchell and the late Cynthia Mitchell. Hotel Galvez is widely known for its longstanding and tasty Sunday Champagne Brunch.

Whiskey Brownies

1/4 cup whiskey

1/4 cup semisweet chocolate chips

1 1/2 cups all-purpose flour

1/2 cup baking cocoa

1 teaspoon baking powder

1/2 teaspoon salt

1 1/3 cups sugar

6 tablespoons butter, softened

1/2 teaspoon vanilla extract

2 eggs

Bring the whiskey to a boil in a small saucepan. Remove from the heat. Add the chocolate chips and stir until melted. Mix the flour, baking cocoa, baking powder and salt together. Beat the sugar and butter in a large mixing bowl at medium speed until light and fluffy. Add the vanilla and eggs and mix well. Add the flour mixture and whiskey mixture and beat at low speed until mixed. Spoon into a 9×9-inch baking pan coated with nonstick cooking spray. Bake in a preheated 350-degree oven for 30 minutes or until the edges pull from the sides of the pan.

Serves 8

Chocolate Chunk Pecan Bars

1 1/2 cups all-purpose flour

2 tablespoons butter, melted

1/4 cup packed brown sugar

3 eggs

3/4 cup light or dark corn syrup

3/4 cup granulated sugar

1/2 cup (1 stick) butter, softened

1 teaspoon vanilla extract

1 1/2 cups chopped pecans

1 3/4 cups chocolate chunks

Beat the flour, 2 tablespoons butter and the brown sugar in a bowl until crumbly. Press in a greased 9×13-inch baking pan. Bake in a preheated 350-degree oven for 14 minutes or until light brown. Remove from the oven. Maintain the oven temperature.

Whisk the eggs, corn syrup, granulated sugar, 1/2 cup butter and the vanilla in a bowl. Stir in the pecans and chocolate chunks. Pour evenly over the crust. Bake for 30 minutes or until set. Cool in the pan on a wire rack. Cut into bars. Serve alone or slightly warmed with ice cream.

Serves 6

Cream Cheese Bars

1/2 cup (1 stick) butter or margarine, melted
1 egg, beaten
1 (2-layer) package yellow cake mix
8 ounces cream cheese, softened
2 eggs
1 cup packed brown sugar
1/2 cup confectioners' sugar
1 teaspoon vanilla extract
Confectioners' sugar for sprinkling (optional)

Combine the butter, one egg and the cake mix in a bowl and mix well. Spread in a greased 9×13-inch baking pan. Beat the cream cheese, two eggs, the brown sugar, 1/2 cup confectioners' sugar and the vanilla in a mixing bowl until smooth. Spread over the cake mix layer. Bake in a preheated 325-degree oven for 45 minutes or until golden brown on top. Sprinkle with additional confectioners' sugar. Cool completely before cutting into bars.

Makes 4 dozen

Lemon Bars

1/2 cup confectioners' sugar
2 cups all-purpose flour
1/2 teaspoon kosher salt
1 cup (2 sticks) unsalted butter, cubed and softened
4 eggs
2 cups granulated sugar
1/2 teaspoon salt
Zest of 1 lemon
1/2 cup fresh lemon juice
1 teaspoon baking powder
1 1/2 tablespoons all-purpose flour
Confectioners' sugar for sprinkling

Mix 1/2 cup confectioners' sugar, 2 cups flour and 1/2 teaspoon kosher salt in a mixing bowl. Add the butter gradually, beating constantly to form a dough. Press in a 9×13-inch baking dish sprayed with nonstick cooking spray. Bake in a preheated 350-degree oven for 20 minutes or until the crust is just beginning to brown around the edges. Reduce the oven temperature to 325 degrees.

Combine the eggs, granulated sugar, 1/2 teaspoon salt, the lemon zest, lemon juice, baking powder and 1 1/2 tablespoons flour in a mixing bowl and beat well. Spread over the hot crust. Bake for 30 minutes. Remove from the oven and cool for 1 hour. Cut into bars and sprinkle with additional confectioners' sugar.

Makes 16 large bars or 24 small bars

Almond Dreams

Cookies

3 1/2 cups all-purpose flour

1 tablespoon baking powder

1/2 teaspoon salt

1 cup (2 sticks) butter, softened

2 cups sugar

3 eggs, beaten

1 teaspoon almond extract

4 drops of red food coloring

Almond Glaze

1 cup (or more) confectioners' sugar

2 tablespoons (or more) half-and-half

1 teaspoon almond extract

To prepare the cookies, mix the flour, baking powder and salt together. Cream the butter and sugar in a mixing bowl. Add the eggs and almond extract and mix well. Beat in the flour mixture. Add the food coloring and mix lightly to marbleize the dough. Chill or freeze the dough until stiff. Roll the dough into small balls and place on an ungreased cookie sheet. Bake in a preheated 350-degree oven for 10 to 12 minutes or until light brown. Remove to a wire rack to cool completely.

To prepare the glaze, combine the confectioners' sugar, half-and-half and almond extract in a bowl and mix until of a pourable consistency, adding additional confectioners' or half-and-half if needed. Spoon over the cooled cookies to glaze.

Makes 56 cookies

Lollipop Cookies

2 3/4 cups all-purpose flour
1 teaspoon baking soda
1/2 teaspoon baking powder
1/4 teaspoon salt
1 cup (2 sticks) unsalted butter, softened

1 cup granulated sugar
1 egg
2 teaspoons vanilla extract
Colored sugar or sprinkles

Whisk the flour, baking soda, baking powder and salt in a bowl. Beat the butter and granulated sugar in a mixing bowl until light and fluffy. Add the egg and vanilla and beat well. Add the flour mixture. Beat at low speed just until mixed. Do not overmix. Place two or three different colors of sugar in separate shallow dishes. Shape 1 1/2 tablespoons of the dough at a time into a ball. Roll each ball in the colored sugar to coat completely, pressing lightly to adhere. Insert a wooden popsicle stick in the center of each ball. Place 1 1/2 inches apart on a cookie sheet with the wooden sticks lying horizontally. Press each ball lightly with the bottom of a glass to flatten slightly. Bake in a preheated 350-degree oven for 20 to 25 minutes or until the edges are light golden brown and crisp. Remove to a wire rack to cool completely. Wrap each cookie individually in colored cellophane bags that coordinate with the color of sugar used.

Makes 2 dozen

Snickerdoodles

7 cups all-purpose flour
2 teaspoons baking soda
1 1/2 tablespoons cinnamon
2 cups (4 sticks) margarine, softened

2 cups packed light brown sugar
2 cups granulated sugar
4 eggs
4 cups pecans, chopped

Sift the flour, baking soda and cinnamon together. Cream the margarine, brown sugar and granulated sugar in a mixing bowl until light and fluffy. Add the eggs and mix well. Stir in the flour mixture and pecans. The dough should be very stiff. Roll the dough into small logs the width of a cookie sheet. Wrap in waxed paper and freeze in the freezer for up to 6 months. Cut into 1/4-inch slices and place on a nonstick cookie sheet. Bake in a preheated 350-degree oven for 15 minutes or until light brown. Remove to a wire rack to cool.

Makes 70 cookies

Crispy Salted White Chocolate Oatmeal Cookies

1 cup all-purpose flour
3/4 teaspoon baking powder
1/2 teaspoon baking soda
1/4 teaspoon salt
3/4 cup plus 2 tablespoons salted butter, softened slightly
1 cup granulated sugar
1/4 cup packed light brown sugar
1 egg
1 teaspoon vanilla extract
2 1/2 cups old-fashioned rolled oats
6 ounces good-quality white chocolate, chopped
1/2 teaspoon flaky sea salt

Whisk the flour, baking powder, baking soda and 1/2 teaspoon salt in a medium bowl. Beat the butter, granulated sugar and brown sugar in a mixing bowl until light and fluffy. Scrape down the side of the bowl with a rubber spatula. Add the egg and vanilla and mix well. Scrape down the side of the bowl again. Add the flour mixture gradually, beating just until mixed after each addition. Add the oats and white chocolate gradually, beating just until mixed after each addition.

Divide the dough into twenty-four equal portions. Each portion should be about 2 tablespoons. Roll each portion between the palms of your hands into balls. Place 2 1/2 inches apart on a cookie sheet lined with baking parchment. Press each ball down gently to about 3/4 inch thick. Sprinkle each with a flake or two of the sea salt. Bake in a preheated 350-degree oven for 13 to 16 minutes or until deep golden brown, rotating the cookie sheet halfway through the baking process. Remove to a wire rack to cool. Do not omit the sea salt and do not use white chocolate chips in this recipe.

Makes 2 dozen

Frosted Sugar Cookies

Cookies

1 1/2 cups (3 sticks) butter, softened
2 cups granulated sugar
1/2 cup confectioners' sugar
4 eggs
2 teaspoons vanilla extract
5 cups all-purpose flour
2 teaspoons baking powder
1 teaspoon salt

Vanilla Frosting

1/2 cup (1 stick) butter, softened
4 cups confectioners' sugar
5 tablespoons milk
1 teaspoon vanilla extract
Food coloring (optional)

To prepare the cookies, cream the butter, granulated sugar and confectioners' sugar in a mixing bowl. Beat in the eggs and vanilla. Stir in the flour, baking powder and salt. Chill, covered, for 2 hours or freeze, covered, for 1 hour. Roll the dough on a floured surface to 1/4 to 1/2 inch thick. Cut into the desired shapes. Place 1 inch apart on a cookie sheet lined with baking parchment. Bake in a preheated 400-degree oven for 6 to 8 minutes or just until the edges are golden brown. Remove to a wire rack to cool completely.

To prepare the frosting, cream the butter in a mixing bowl until smooth. Add the confectioners' sugar gradually, beating constantly. Add the milk and vanilla and beat well. Tint with food coloring. Spread over the cooled cookies. Let stand for 30 to 60 minutes or until the frosting is set before storing in an airtight container.

Makes about 5 dozen

Pecan Biscotti

4 cups all-purpose flour
1/4 teaspoon salt
1 teaspoon baking powder
1/2 cup (1 stick) butter, softened
1 1/2 cups sugar

2 tablespoons rinsed anise seeds
1 cup chopped pecans
4 eggs, beaten

Sift the flour, salt and baking powder together. Beat the butter and sugar in a mixing bowl until creamy. Add the anise seeds and pecans. Stir in the flour mixture. Add the eggs and mix well. Divide the dough into two equal portions. Shape each portion into a log. Wrap in plastic wrap. Chill for 8 to 10 hours. Unwrap the logs and place on a greased cookie sheet. Bake in a preheated 325-degree oven for 45 minutes or until golden brown. Cool on a wire rack. Cut each log into slices. For an extra-crunchy cookie, place the sliced cookies on a cookie sheet and bake for 5 to 10 minutes longer.

Makes 2 dozen

Perfect Pecan Pralines

1 cup buttermilk
3 cups sugar
1 teaspoon baking soda
1/4 teaspoon salt

2 cups or more chopped pecans
1 teaspoon vanilla extract
2 tablespoons butter

Combine the buttermilk, sugar, baking soda and salt in a large saucepan. Bring to a boil. Cook to 234 degrees on a candy thermometer, soft-ball stage. Remove from the heat. Add the pecans, vanilla and butter. Return to the heat. Return to 234 degrees on a candy thermometer, soft-ball stage. Remove from the heat. Beat until the candy loses its gloss, thickens and looks creamy. Drop by teaspoonfuls onto heavy-duty foil, working quickly. Let stand until set.

Makes 2 1/2 to 3 pounds

Tropical Cinnamon Chips

Cinnamon Chips
4 (7-inch) flour tortillas
1 tablespoon sugar
1/2 teaspoon cinnamon

Tropical Salsa
2 Granny Smith apples, peeled and chopped
1 cup strawberries, chopped
1 kiwifruit, chopped
Zest and juice of 1 small orange
2 tablespoons brown sugar
2 tablespoons apple jelly

To prepare the chips, spray the tortillas lightly with nonstick cooking spray. Sprinkle with a mixture of the sugar and cinnamon. Cut each tortilla into eight wedges using a pizza cutter. Place in a single layer on a round baking stone or baking sheet. Bake in a preheated 400-degree oven for 8 to 10 minutes or until light brown and crisp. Remove to a wire rack to cool completely.

To prepare the salsa, combine the apples, strawberries and kiwifruit in a 1-quart bowl. Add the orange zest, orange juice, brown sugar and apple jelly and mix gently. Serve with the cinnamon chips.

Serves 10 to 12

BISHOP'S PALACE

The Bishop's Palace is designated as a National Historic Landmark in Galveston. It is located on the corner of 14th Street and Broadway. It was built from 1887 to 1892 for Colonel Walter Gresham and his family. Gresham was the founder of the Gulf, Colorado, and Santa Fe Railroad and also served in the Texas Legislature. This 7,500-square-foot building is constructed of steel and stone and has unique Tudor arches and a variety of carvings.

That's Amore!

A Menu for an
Authentic Italian Dinner

Appetizer
Spinach Italian Tarts 43

Salad
Italian Bruschetta Salad 67

Bread
Rosemary Focaccia 73

Entrée
Classic Lasagna 116

Side Dish
Eggplant Parmesan 151

Dessert
Almond Dreams 186

Extending Our Appreciation to...

Bill Glenn

Abbey Hanson

Hayley Hardcastle

Maceo Spice & Import Company

Robert Mihovil

Sandy Starr

Cindy Sullivan

Sarah Sullivan

The past and present active members, sustainers,
and provisional classes for all of your countless efforts
and contributions in making this cookbook
a successful accomplishment for
The Junior League of Galveston County.

2006—2010 Cookbook Committees

Our sincere apologies to anyone who contributed to
Culinary Classics from Beachside to Boardwalk
that we may have unintentionally omitted.

Contributors

Kathy Adams
Lynda Adams
Gloria Adriance-Ansell
Pam Alexander
Mari Allmond
Ann Anderson
Cristina Anderson
Kendra Anderson
Martha Angell
Libbie Ansell
Karen Apffel
Selena Apffel
Christine Arcari
Brenda Atchley
Swati Athavale
Dorothea Balentine
Amineh Baradar
Mary Beth Bassett
Carole Bell
Diana Bertini
Erin Best
Judy Biggs
Jenna Black
Mary Bolger
Emily Bonnecaze
Lindsey Boone
Larissa Botik
Linda Brack
Lawren Bradford
Reene Bradshaw
Tammy Brindley
Christen Brokaw
Susan Broll
Roserika Brooks
Amy Brown
Angie Brown
Margaret Brown

Cynthia Buckley
Betty Bunce
Terri Burchfield
Jennifer Burnett
Robyn Bushong
Mary Jane Caddell
Jennifer Caffey
Alicia Cahill
Mary Lee Cambiano
Connie Campbell
Deborah Candelari
Lori Carnes
Mary Castillo
Melanie Caufman
Susan Cecelia
Sheyanne Chan
Beth Chavarria
Jennifer Chiles
Ellen Chuoke
Debby Citti
Betsy Clardy
Valeria Clarke
Patricia Clason
Carolyn Clyburn
Kim Colombo
Gabriella Cone
Ruth Cook
Saundra Cook
Virginia Cook
Mary Elizabeth Cooper
Franka Correia
Margaret Sissy Couvillion
Joy Cowan
Susie Cowher
Kate Cox
Bea Craig
Lori Crossno

Molly Crow
Martha Cuenod
Stevy Curbow
Amanda Daigle
Mary Dalbey
Dianne Dale
Kathryn Daniel
Amber Darrow
Elisabeth Darst
Anouk Davis
Barbara Davis
Cynthia Davis
Frances Davis
Karen Davis
Laurie DeClaire
Joanie Deis
Adriane dela Cruz
Faye Derbes
Karen DeVoy
Anne DeWitt
Francis Dibrell
Peggy Dietel
Felicity Dodson
Levon Doggett
Lisa Doguet
Michelle Doguet
Rebekah Doherty
Wendy Dohm
Judy Dolfi
Linda Dolfi
Jennifer Dominguez
Lori Douglas
Debra Doyle
Stephanie Doyle
Wendy Drapela
Jean Driscoll
Dina Driskill

Ellen Druss
Nicole Duckett
Susan Duif
Ashlee DuPont
Peggy DuPont
Ashley Dusek
Chris Dykstra
Susan Eckel
Elizabeth Edmunds
Cindy Ervin-Cagle
Betty Eskridge
Erica Eskuchen
Dedra Etzel
Karen Ann Evers
Sandee Fairey
Julius Falk
Angelina Farella, M.D.
Janet Farmer
Ted Farmer
Susan Fieglein
Ashlyn Fitch
Cathy Fitch
Mildred Balderachi Fitzsimmons
Karen Flowers
Meagan Flynn
Shelly Fordyce
Jill Forschler
Carolyn Foutch
Tobi Frankfather
Marjorie Frantz
Theresa French
Stacey Frescura
Pam Froeschner
Dorris Fuchs
Sally Futch
Pamela Gabriel
Amanda Gaido
Carolyn Gaido
Sally Galbraith

Gloria Gallo
Kristi Gann
Catherine Garrison
Kriste Garrison
Kris Garza
Samantha Geraci
Gina Gilmore
Lynsey Ginsberg
Alyssa Gisler
Carolyn Gisler
Kathy Glass
Bill Glenn
Doryn Glenn
Sara Glenn
Dori Golan
Michelle Gordon
Lauraleigh Gourley-Vogel
Victoria Green
Lourdes Gregory, R.Ph.
Susan Gregory
Neysa Gremillion
Virginia Grief
Camille Haglund
Lauren Hall
Erica Hallmark
Elizabeth Hanlon
Abbey Hanson
Kristen Hanson
Linda Hanson
Ron Hanson
Tiffany Hanson
Hayley Hardcastle
Mandy Hardee
Edie Harrington
Laurel Hartman
Amanda Hawes
Michele Hay
Erin Haynes
Doris Heard

Dorothy Henderson
Shaye Henderson
Melissa Henry
Liz Henson
Debi Herren
B. J. Herz
Michelle Hicks
Ronit Hicks
Holli Hirsch
Joanne Hlavenka
Amy Hoff
Claudette Hoffman
Janet Hoffman
Michelle Holland
Patricia Holleman
Christine Hopkins
Nan Hornbeck
Gerry Hornstein
Lori Hoskins
Marcia Hutchings
Lauren Huxel
Joan Hyatt
Kristen Hyder
Coleena Jackson
Liz Jackson
Jeannie Janota
Rebecca Jaworski
Kathryn Jenkins
Christi Jensen
Kelly Johns
Lori Johnson
Pennie Johnson
Deborah Jones
Rhoda Jones
Terry Lynn Jones
Jill Kaale
Sara Kana
Melanie Kaufman
Donna Kearney

Erin Kearney-Conrad
Rachel Keehn
Amanda Keelen
Katherine Kelso
Hetta Kempner
Sandra Kim
Patricia Kirby
Michele Klump
Cathy Knecht
Marjorie Kovacevich
Cara Koza
Roxann Kriticos
Jennifer Kubeczka
Tracey Kuhlow
Marjorie Kusnerik
Kathleen Kyle
Brenda Lacombe
Colleen Laine
Tonka Lane
Sue Langston
Inez Lasel
M'Linda Lasswell
Hartman Laurel
Saralin Lawder
Ann Leahy
Linda Leck
Brandy Lecoq
Shannon Lecoq
Phu Leimer
Trisha Leimer
Kristen Lepo
Bob Lewis
Vicki Lewis
Emily Lindberg
Ruby Litton
Jane Loomis
Dixie Louis
Barbara Lund
Janet Lydick

Cindi Lyons
Linda Macdonald
Kimberly Mack
Karen Madden
Andrea Madison
Diane Magliolo
Rachel Mallernee
Shana Marcon
Barbara Markey
Raegan Markey
Meredith Martin
Jessica Martinez
Mari Martinez
Ann Masel
Meredith Masel
Annie Matthews
Cynthia Matthews
Ann McAfee
Elizabeth McCarty
Dr. T. C. McCormick
Maureen McCutchen
Lola McDaniel
Serina McEntire
Joan McLeod
Heather McMillian
Vanessa Medellin
Judy Meier
Donna Mencacci
Rondell Merritt
Olivia Meyer
Lydia Michel
Lisa Mignerey
Robert Mihovil
Phyllis Milstein
Kathryn Mixon
Debby Molloy
Gayle Monsour
Heather Monteleone
Stacey Moreno

Laura Morrison
Ida Jo Morse
Ellen Mosher
Brenda Moulton
Jennifer Murray
Patricia Murray
Keri Myers
Nita Myers
Kim Mytelka
Joy Nagel
Judy Nagel
Linda Nathan
Dedde Nations
Amy Neblett
Pam Nelson
Harriet Newding
Melanie Noble
Wendy O'Donohoe
Kerry O'Malley
Monica Ott
Kelly Panfilli
Addie Pappous
Kathryn Parks
Amber Pastusek
Maureen Patton
Maggie Pearson
Holly Pelletier
Becky Penton
Lindsay Perez
Pamela Petty
Sara Pfeifer
Samantha Pitman
Gayle Plackemeier
Jeannie Poirier
Karen Porter
Kathryn Potter
Kay Potts
Constance Powel
Kimberly Primm

Dianna Puccetti
Jimmy Puccetti
Marilyn Puffer
Eliza Quigley
Sharon Raimer
Peggy Rapp
Ronnie Rapp
Kimblyn Raschke
Leila Ravandi
Stephanie Regitz
Mary Ann Reilly
Mary Remmers
Sue Rice
Gwyn Richardson, M.D.
Gail Rider
Susan Rismiller
Diane Roane
Paula Roberts
Laura Roffmann
Elizabeth Rogers
James E. Rogers
Maryanne Rogers
Brooke Saldana
Cindy Sapio
Melody Saueressig
Betty Schnake
Katie Schuler
Cindy Schulz
Gretchen Schulz
Yvette Schulz
Erin Schutmaat
Margaret Scofelia
Elizabeth Seidel
Heidi Seigel
Sandra Seinsheimer
Kay Serafin
Suzanne Sexton
Carrie Shannon
Linda Sheehan

Elizabeth Shelton
Tesa Skipper
Sarah Smith
Erika Speer
Valleri Speer
Sandy Starr
Katherine Stathakos
Stephanie Stathakos
Jill Stephenson
Pamela Stevens
Michelle Stokes
Alice Stone
Cindy Sullivan
Jocelyn Sullivan
Sarah Sullivan
Susanne Sullivan
Andrea Sunseri
Carolyn Sunseri
Dana Swan
Kerri Sweeney
Denise Taller
Christy Taylor
Donna Teichman
Kathy Templeton
Jill Termini
Lori Termini-Kline
Gina Thomas
Kelly Thompson
Leonora Thompson
Diane Thornton
Lori Tieken
Kimberly Tindel
Erin Toberman
Dana Todd
Mary Lou Torregrossa
Jeri Tosio
Mary Townsend
Kathy Tramonte
Sarah Trombley

Mary Uher
K. Urabee
Jennie Urban
Cassie Vanderford
Jan Vanderpool
Kathy Varbec
Stephanie Caravageli Vasut
Rina Vintz
Kimberley Walker
Ruth Walsh
Murleen Ware
Judy Watkins
Amy Weber
Sue Weber
Kristi Wees
Kelsi Wegner
Joan Weil
Leslie Welch
Carol Wells
Gina Welsh
Teri Wenglein-Callender
Mandy Wesley
Amy Whitmore
Patricia Whittington
Evangeline Whorton
Patience Wildenfels
Jennifer Wilkins
Sheridan Willey
Patricia Williams
Susan Williams
Dorothy Wolma
Kim Woods
Elise Worthen
Susan Worthen
Paige Worthington
Kristi Wright
Carol Yarbrough
Janis Yarbrough
Molly Zolas, M.D.

Resources

www.artistboat.org

www.artshound.com/event/detail/29571

www.balineseroom.net

www.bayouwildlifepark.com

www.bayreef.com

www.bolivarchamber.org

www.butlerlonghornmuseumandheritagepark.com

www.citytowninfo.com/places/texas/dickinson

www.crystalbeach.com/chamber.html

www.galveston.com

www.galvestonbirdsers.com

www.galvestonhistory.org

www.galvestonislandstatepark.org

www.harbourplayhouse.com

www.harvestmoonregatta.com

www.jazzhouston.com/articles/words/kemah

www.jlgalveston.org

www.kemah.net

www.leaguecitychamber.com

www.mardigrasgalveston.com

www.moodymansion.org

www.murdochspier.com

www.portofgalveston.com

www.sacredheartgalveston.org

www.tcyc.org

www.texasbob.com/travel/tbt-bolivarferry.html

www.texas-city_tx.org/rectour.com

www.thegrand.com

www.tsm-elissa.org

Photography Index

Index